NORFOLK

A Changing Countryside
1780~1914

Contract sheep dippers at work in the early years of the present century.

NORFOLK
A Changing Countryside
1780~1914

Susanna Wade Martins

Phillimore

1988

Published by
PHILLIMORE & CO. LTD.
Shopwyke Hall, Chichester, Sussex

ISBN 0 85033 656 2

Printed and bound in Great Britain by
RICHARD CLAY LTD.
Chichester, Sussex

Contents

List of Illustrations

Frontispiece: Contract sheep dippers

Acknowledgements

This book is the result of 17 years spent in Norfolk working on various aspects of its modern history, during which time I have received help from a wide variety of people. The staff of the Norfolk Record Office, the Local Studies Library and the Norfolk Rural Life Museum, Gressenhall, have all given a great deal of assistance, particularly in the selection of illustrations. This type of study relies heavily on field work and owners of farms and houses have always been very welcoming and helpful when I have visited them. The older inhabitants have always been very patient and generous with their time when explaining how things were in the past.

I am also grateful to the following for permission to reproduce illustrations: Bodleian Library, Oxford, 19 and 20; Lady Cholmondeley, 57; The Fakenham Town Gasworks Museum Trust, 88; Peter R. Fox, 86 and 87a-d; Sir Thomas Hare, Stow Estate, 30; Hethersett Women's Institute, 31, 43, 47 and 92; C. Middleton, 7, 34, 48, 49 and 50; The National Trust, 16; Norfolk County Council, Local Studies Library, 44, 78, 79, 91 and 93; Norfolk Historic Farm Buildings Survey, 11, 37 and 96; Norfolk Museums Service (Bridewell Museum, Norwich, 1, 3 and 4; Norfolk Rural Life Museum, Gressenhall, 17, 33, 35, 39, 40, 41, 45, 46, 55, 56, 64, 73, 75, 83, 97, 98 and 99); the R.A.F. (Crown Copyright), 5; Royal Commission on the Historical Monuments of England, 12, 70, 71 and 72; Swaffham Parochial Church Council, 89; H. Swales, 80 and 81; Trustees of the 7th Lord Suffield Will Trust, 9 and 10.

Chapter One

Introduction

National history as much as local conditions ensured that the Norfolk countryside changed more in the 120 years following the French Revolution than in any comparable period before. Britain was changing from an agricultural to an industrial nation, and Norfolk, although right on the fringe of the new developments, was still affected; as a result its role in the national economy was reversed.

In the Middle Ages Norfolk had been the most densely populated county in England, and Norwich the second city to London. Before 1750 Norfolk had been an 'industrial' county. Daniel Defoe described in 1722 the populous villages where there was work for all, even the children over three years old, helping in the spinning and weaving of yarn. Norwich itself was the centre of this trade and by the 18th century most of the weavers were based there. Cloth was produced by these craftsmen, both for the home market and for export. Agriculture was also prosperous, not only providing the raw material for the woollen industry, but also corn which was exported from the Norfolk ports.

While industry remained based on locally-grown raw materials and on the skill of craftsmen, Norfolk prospered, but by the late 18th century this was beginning to change. Raw cotton was imported from India and America through the Atlantic ports of Liverpool and Glasgow and began to compete with wool as a fashionable textile. Water-powered machines began to take over, firstly from the spinners and then the weavers, but Norfolk had no fast flowing rivers suited to the establishment of mills. Later, steam power increased in importance and again Norfolk could not compete as there were no local coal deposits and so it was West Yorkshire and Lancashire that gained by the innovations. The decline and final demise of handloom weaving in Norfolk was slow. Norwich firms diversified into making types of cloth which could not yet be made on machines. The complex patterns of Norwich shawls and silk crêpe could not be mass-produced and the embroidery on many Norwich shawls had to be added by hand. The discontent of the many handloom weavers as they found their work gradually slipping away from them in the 1830s is shown by their support for the Chartist movement. Although crêpe, silk and horse hair continued to be produced until after the end of the 19th century, the days of Norwich as a major centre of the textile industry were really over by 1800.

However, if the fortunes of the spinners and weavers were in decline, those of the farmers were greatly increased by the 'Industrial Revolution'. As the industrial towns grew and more and more people from the countryside moved into them, this new urban population needed feeding. The years of Napoleon's Continental Blockade at the beginning of the 19th century meant that Britain's food had to be produced at home and this added to the demand for produce from the farmers. The best wheat and barley lands in England are in East Anglia and so Norfolk farmers were well placed to meet these needs. Grain was no longer exported, but sold on the home market and the famine prices of the Napoleonic wars allowed for an increasingly wealthy agricultural society.

1. Detail of a mid-19th-century Norwich 'fillover shawl'. Both the cloth and the pattern are machine woven.

2. Silk mill built by Norwich Yarn Company in 1839.

 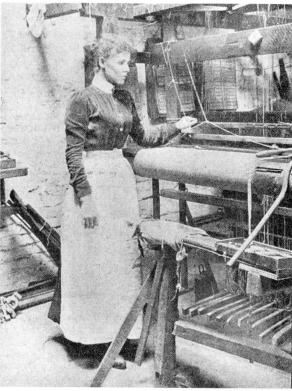

3. & 4. Silk weaving continued in Norwich into the 20th century and these two pictures, published in 1902 in the *Gentlewomen's Magazine*, show workers at James Arnold's mill in Cherry Lane, off Pitt Street.

Farmers became prosperous as craft industries declined and Norfolk changed from an industrial county trading eastwards into northern Europe, to an agricultural one serving the needs of the home market.

This change is reflected in the landscape. While many Norfolk market towns stagnated, allowing their elegant Georgian market places to remain little changed to this day, the countryside was greatly altered. The last of the strip fields surviving from the Middle Ages disappeared as the large landowners endeavoured to create compact efficient farms that would bring in good rents from progressive farmers prepared to experiment with the new techniques being developed. More important was the enclosure of commons. As late as 1790, large areas of common land still survived in Norfolk, but by the end of the Napoleonic wars nearly all except those on the lightest and poorest soils had been enclosed. The work of allocating land was carried out by enclosure commissioners who divided the commons amongst the farms according to the grazing rights that went with them. If all these farms were owned by the same landlord and farmed by tenants, the landscape could be completely reorganised into carefully laid out regular fields transected by straight enclosure roads, often with new farmsteads

5. This aerial photograph shows the village of Warham in the north (*bottom*) and the river Stiffkey meandering through watermeadows across the west (*right*) of the photograph. The central area is taken up with large rectangular fields: those to the west of the road were laid out as part of the late 18th-century enclosures. Typical of this period of rearrangement is the field barn to the south of the wood and approached by a straight access road. To the east (*left*), the fields are less regular and the double right-angle bends in some of the hedgerows indicate the survival of old strip boundaries.

built in the middle of the farmland they served. The size of these substantial farmsteads, especially the house and barn, is an indication of the prosperity of farming and the importance of the grain crop. Changes in the landscape of the scale experienced during this period have not been repeated until the post-war destruction of hedgerows during the last 30 years.

6. A substantial Victorian farmhouse near Dereham.

As the 19th century progressed, Norfolk maintained its position as England's foremost agricultural county. The Napoleonic wars were followed by years of depression as agriculture reorganised itself on a peace-time footing. Declining local industries and an increasing population meant that unemployment was high and wages low. Riots and machine breaking were frequent, but by the late 1830s things were improving and the period from then until the 1870s is often called the 'Golden Age of English farming'. The 'high farming' techniques developed at this time led to improved yields of grain and an increased quality and quantity of livestock which, after the arrival of the railways, could easily be transported to market. Farm buildings were extended to serve the new needs and the last of the commons were enclosed. Optimism within the farming community was high. The belief that production would increase as knowledge increased and that there was an insatiable demand for food which would prevent prices falling was the basic philosophy of 'high farming'. These prosperous farmers needed machinery and, later, feeds and fertilisers. Market towns, particularly those on railway lines, were able to benefit from the situation. Maltings, iron foundries and feed mills were to be found in nearly all of them by 1870.

From 1870, the situation began to change yet again. As the prairies of the United States and Canada were opened up, cheap grain began to be shipped across the Atlantic to Britain and British farmers began to suffer. Those with mixed farming systems, where livestock was important, fared best, but much land in Norfolk, as elsewhere, went out of continual cultivation and instead was put down to pasture and only ploughed up every few years. This less intensive system required fewer labourers and so hastened the decline in village population which had already begun. However, while horses were still the main source of motive power on the farms, the number of farm workers remained high by present-day standards. Until 1850 the population of rural areas continued to grow, but after that the villages began to decline as people moved off to the towns, both within the county and further afield.

A declining workforce and a depressed agriculture meant that the countryside began to look very different. Hedges were not trimmed so regularly nor gates mended and painted. Drains and ditches were left uncleaned and farm buildings were not repaired. Except on the best run estates, especially those enjoying an income from outside agriculture, the land had a neglected air. This was in great contrast to the situation mid-century when well-tilled, weed-free fields, neatly laid hedges and comfortable farmhouses had given an impression of prosperity and stability; the natural consequence of good management.

By the end of the century, farming had settled down into a new, less intensive system. Farmers no longer had the confidence they had mid century; however, by relying less on their cereals, reducing costs and growing new crops such as soft fruit and vegetables, and later, sugar beet, they were able to adapt to new situations. Rents

7. Village carpenters remained essential members of the community well into this century. Sam Day, shown here in his apron and with his saw, was photographed in Weybourne in 1852.

also had to drop and, as a result of declining incomes, many houses of the gentry were locked up or let to wealthy industrialists for the shooting season.

The appearance of villages also changed during the last years of the century. Many of the worst cottages were abandoned while land owners were at last building cottages more suited to human habitation. Every village had a school by 1880 and nonconformist chapels were springing up everywhere.

While new buildings appeared, some of the old craftsmen were disappearing as more goods were factory-produced; improved transport meant that more goods were available in local towns. Village tailors, hatters and potters were amongst the first to go. Coopers were no longer needed as metal buckets replaced wooden ones and breweries were only to be found in towns. Cobblers were reduced in numbers and, as factory shoes replaced hand-made ones, they became menders rather than makers of shoes. The harness maker, wheelwright, saddler and blacksmith remained a familiar sight in most villages until the 1940s and a wide range of retail shops survived, disappearing only with the arrival of the motor car. While cheap food meant lower profits for the farmers, it allowed for an improvement in farm workers' standards of living and meant that some of the worst rural conditions began to disappear.

The 19th century was therefore a century of change. Norfolk ceased to be an area producing what had been Britain's most valuable export (woollen textiles) and instead became the nation's granary. This role was challenged in the 1870s with the importation of wheat from across the Atlantic, and Norfolk farmers had to adjust again to suit the times. Much new land which had been ploughed up earlier in the century reverted to semi-permanent pasture. Villages changed and declined as the majority of the population ceased to live in the countryside. The role of the market and railway town grew whilst that of the village decreased in importance. Manufactured goods reached the country and farm labourers, their standard of living now slowly rising, were able to afford a few luxuries. Universal education was now at last beginning to combat illiteracy and, after 1884, rural labourers were allowed to vote. The increasing availability of newspapers meant that political awareness was growing.

There was change, but there was also continuity. Village society seemed stable with the institutions of the great house and church still firmly in control. While horses worked the land, farming and farming tasks continued very much as before. If the shifting basis of Norfolk's economy and development, resulting from the agricultural and industrial revolutions, was the predominant theme of the 19th century, the greatest social changes were delayed until after the First World War.

Chapter Two

The Great House and the Gentry

Although much changed in 19th-century Norfolk, one of the most stable elements in the countryside was the Great House and the life around it. Over half of the county was owned by landowners with more than 1,000 acres and, although some of the owners were institutions such as Cambridge colleges, most were local families, making their homes within the county. Many of their houses, usually standing within a park, still survive. Two hundred and twenty five families owned more than 1,000 acres while 335 'seats of nobility, clergy and gentry' are listed in the 1881 *Directory*.

8.   East Bilney Hall, now run as a nursing home, stands within a small park. It was the home of the Collisons, owners of an estate of between 1,200 and 1,500 acres. They also controlled the appointment of the rector of Bilney and Beetley who was often a member of the family.

The most impressive mansions and largest parks belonged, not surprisingly, to the owners of the largest estates. At 40,000 acres, the estate of the Coke family (Earls of Leicester from 1837) was by far the largest. Its land was mainly in north-west Norfolk, centred on the impressive Palladian mansion at Holkham. Built over a period of 30 years from 1734, it was designed partly by one of the greatest architects of the day,

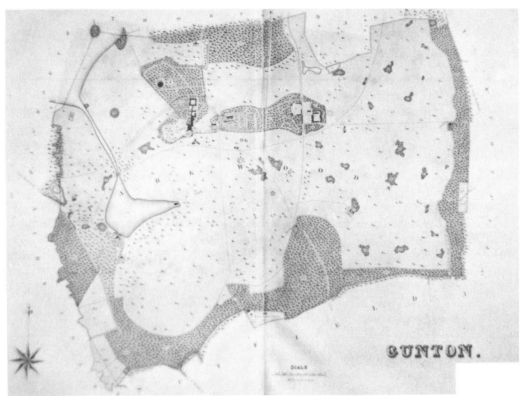

9. & 10. These two maps of Gunton Park, drawn in 1784 and 1835, show the changes made in the landscape around the hall over a period of 50 years. The earlier map shows a formal layout of avenues and vistas which had been thinned out and 'naturalised' by 1835. A new area of woods surrounding the stables and home farm had been created by '1835 and an area of fields to the west of the lake was brought into the park.

William Kent, as well as by Matthew Brettingham and the owner himself, Thomas Coke. The laying out of the present park was left to his successor, the Whig politician and agricultural improver, Thomas William Coke. Farms were taken in hand, trees planted and the lake improved until, by his death in 1842, it covered 3,000 acres; a belt of trees had been planted all the way round the nine-mile perimeter. The two nearby estates of Houghton and Raynham were next in size to Holkham, being over 18,000 acres each. They were also owned by families who had made their name in 18th-century politics. Robert Walpole, while he was prime minister, commissioned the building of Houghton Hall, designed by Colin Campbell. Raynham Hall, the home of Walpole's fellow Secretary of State, Lord Townshend, is an older and less grandiose building, erected from 1622. The Harbord family, created Lords Suffield in 1786, controlled an estate of similar size in the north-east of the county and built Gunton Hall, designed by Matthew Brettingham, in the years following 1741. The park was the work of a succession of landscapers from Bridgeman to Repton.

All landowners added to their houses and outbuildings during the 19th century, often erecting stable blocks and laying out the formal gardens and parterres so much admired by the Victorians. Some new houses were also built. Bylaugh Hall, now a ruin, was designed by Sir Charles Barry, son of the architect of the Houses of Parliament, and is one of the few entirely new country houses built on a virgin site in the Victorian period. New gardens were created from ploughed fields by W. A. Nesfield. One of the most successful early Victorian landscape gardeners, Nesfield also worked for other Norfolk landowners such as the Earl of Leicester.

In 1873 the Hares rebuilt Stow Hall near Kings Lynn in a grand Elizabethan style. On the slightly smaller south Norfolk estate of Sir R. J. Buxton, the flamboyant S. S. Teulon was employed between 1857 and 1860 to design Shadwell Court and an estate village at Brettenham. The halls at Hillington and Hunstanton are examples of Victorian Gothic and Victorian Jacobean architecture. By far the grandest, however, was the Jacobean-style house built in 1870 by the Prince of Wales on his recently acquired Sandringham estate. The interest taken by all classes of gentry in house building and alteration throughout the 19th century is an indication of their continued prosperity and confidence in the future.

The majority of Norfolk landowners were old county families, many of whom had taken advantage of the Reformation and the sale of monastic lands to amass their estates. Queen Elizabeth I's Chief Justice, Edward Coke, bought up land around his home at Mileham and Tittleshall before expanding into the Holkham area. Another royal servant, this time the Surveyor General to Charles I and II, Sir Charles Harbord, began accumulating the Gunton estate in the 17th century. The Townshends had been a county family of standing before the second Viscount began his political career under Queen Anne. The Walpoles had been local squires for several generations before Robert became a Secretary of State for George I.

There were of course newcomers. For instance, John Ketton, who had made his fortune selling oil cake and other animal feeds, bought Felbrigg in 1863 when the eccentricities of 'mad Windham' had forced the estate onto the market.

The great estates were distributed very unevenly across the county. By far the largest proportion of them were in the north-west, on the light soils of the chalk lands where one could travel a very long way crossing the Raynham, Houghton, Sandringham and

11. Bylaugh Hall was built in the early 1850s to fulfill the terms of a family will and is a rare example of a completely new Victorian house. It was hardly lived in and has been a ruin since 1950 although the stable block and clock tower are still intact.

12. Originally an 18th-century house, Shadwell Court was rebuilt by Sir R. J. Buxton between 1839 and 1855. From 1839-42 Edward Blore, a safe and staid architect, built a new south front in Elizabethan style. The wing to the right-hand side of this photograph is mostly his work. In 1850 S. S. Teulon, one of Victorian England's more extravagant architects, was commissioned to build a new entrance, a huge music room and the tower. Much of the wing to the left was built to his designs.

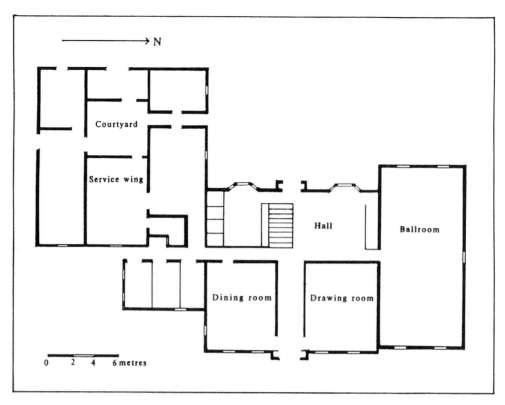

13. & 14. Plan and photograph of the east front of Whitwell Hall, the home of Robert Leamon, a prominent county figure in the early 19th century. Although this house is of several periods, the east front, shown here, was built for Robert Leamon in about 1840. The ballroom to the north (*right*) was also added and the east entrance became the main one. The ha-ha, or brick wall concealed within a ditch to prevent animals grazing in the park wandering onto the gardens near the house, can be seen in the foreground of this photograph. As well as the main rooms shown on the plan, the house also had the usual range of outbuildings, including a walled kitchen garden and conservatory, farm buildings, coach house and a dovecot.

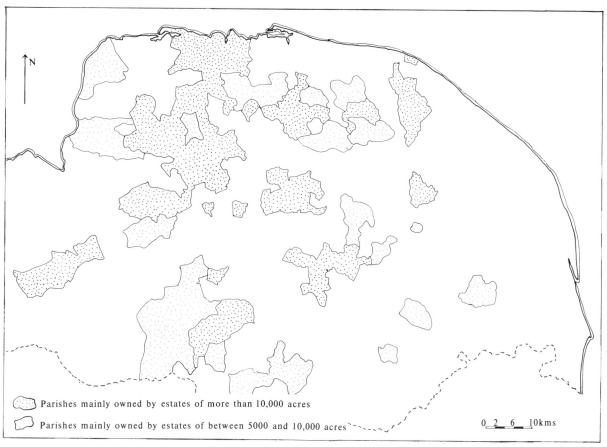

15. Map showing the distribution of land held in estates of over 5,000 acres in 1863. The contrast between the owner-occupiers of the south and east and the estate-dominated north and west is very obvious.

Legend on map:
Parishes mainly owned by estates of more than 10,000 acres
Parishes mainly owned by estates of between 5000 and 10,000 acres
0 2 6 10kms

Holkham estates without ever passing an owner-occupied farm. In the heavy claylands of the south, however, farms were smaller and more frequently owner occupied, or rented from small and often rather badly managed estates; the standard of farming was often much lower in these areas. The estate villages of the north, with their stereotyped semi-detached cottages, their landlord-restored church and sponsored school and, away from the village centre, their farmsteads set in the middle of well arranged fields, contrasted sharply with the majority of the settlements in the south.

Norfolk had been renowned for its lack of landed estates and the independence of its yeoman farmers. However, by the end of the 18th century the situation seems to have changed with William Marshall (1787), Arthur Young (1804) and Nathaniel Kent (1796) all noting that the number of small proprietors was decreasing. There were areas east of Norwich 'where entire parishes which had been farmed by the yeomanry were falling into the hands of men of fortune'.

Although many Norfolk landowners were individualists and made their mark on the national scene in a variety of ways, there were certain interests and duties that were typical of the class as a whole and helped give it solidarity. Of these interests, one of the most important was an almost universal enthusiasm for field sports.

16.   End-page from T. Windham Cremer's game book kept during the 1850s. In his idle moments in the field he sketched a wide variety of both the two- and four-legged participants in the sport.

Shooting had long been a favourite occupation of county society and strict preservation of game began on some estates in the late 18th century. In Norfolk it became far more important in the 19th century, particularly in the last quarter. The number of gamekeepers increased and the semi-tame birds were then driven by beaters until they flew over the fences behind which the shooting parties were ranged. This 'grand battue' sport, typical of the huge shooting parties of Sandringham at the end of the century, was very different from the simple and informal shoots on the Holkham estate 70 years before. Lady Elizabeth Stanhope visited her step-brother, the second Earl of Leicester, for Christmas in 1847. On Christmas eve there was a grand battue and Lady Stanhope reported, 'They are to kill 500 pheasants and 500 hares, which are all to be driven to one spot – a regular massacre. How different from the old days!'. In her father's time, shoots had been held regularly twice a week from the first Wednesday in November throughout the winter. The number of birds shot rose steadily from 1,560 in 1805 to 8,748 in 1901. Coke's political friends had often joined him for the sport and one wonders what, other than pheasants, was discussed on these occassions. Possibly parliamentary tactics were worked out in the coverts around Holkham as well as on the race courses at Newmarket and in the clubs of London.

William Howe Windham, the owner of Felbrigg Hall between 1833 and 1845, took a great interest in the shooting on his estate and the game books, written in his own hand, are full of his own comments on the day's sport. On one occasion he wrote, 'I never shot so well in my life; I killed 7 double shots'. Shooting accidents were as common then as in more recent times. Windham describes one rather minor mishap: 'Billy Lines, in shooting a rat in a fence, stupidly shot off the tail of Simpson's favourite bitch'. The annual bag at Felbrigg at this time was about 4,000.

The grand battue did have its defendants. Rider Haggard, the author of *She* and *King Solomon's Mines*, was an enthusiastic sportsman with a small estate in the south of the county. He wrote in the 1890s, 'Battue shooting, as it is popularly called, is a favourite target for the scorn of people who know very little about it, and to save their lives could not bring down more than one bird in 20. As a matter of fact, it is a difficult art – if anyone doubt it, let him watch Lord Walsingham bringing down pheasant after pheasant, not picking or choosing, but taking them one after another as they come at every possible or impossible angle . . .'.

The preservation of game often meant the destruction of crops and so shooting would lead to ill feeling between the landlord and his tenants. Farms where the landlords' interest in sport took priority over the interests of the tenants could be difficult to let, especially when agricultural incomes were depressed. This was true of a farm within Gunton Park in the 1890s. 'Great care, thought and consideration should be given to it as, being surrounded by woods, it would be called and considered a game farm; consequently applicants have a great hold on the landlord and his agent, saying, It is a game farm – I shall give but a low rent. I think good buildings and houses would counteract that.' When the 3rd Earl Suffield became owner of Gunton he took the unusual step of ordering the gamekeepers to destroy all the hares on the estate and to remove all the spring guns from the woods. On the Sandringham estate matters reached a head soon after the Prince of Wales arrived. Grid iron strips were cut across arable fields and planted for game shelters without the tenants being consulted. Cottages for under-keepers had priority over the needs of farm labourers and the new head-keeper, appointed when the Prince of Wales took over the estate, 'treated every farmer as a poacher'. Finally, Mrs. Cresswell of Appleton killed 71 pheasants in an act of revenge. This was followed by a heated enquiry in which Mrs. Cresswell was cleared. Following the appointment of a new keeper, feelings calmed down.

With the onset of agricultural depression and falling rents at the end of the century, many smaller landlords cut down on the preservation of game. On the other hand, on the poor Breckland soils, sport was now more profitable than agriculture. The gentry moved out and let the shooting to tenants who only came for a few months in the year and took no interest in local affairs. The civil engineer, Edward McKenzie, bought over

17. Gamekeepers in Bylaugh Park about 1907.

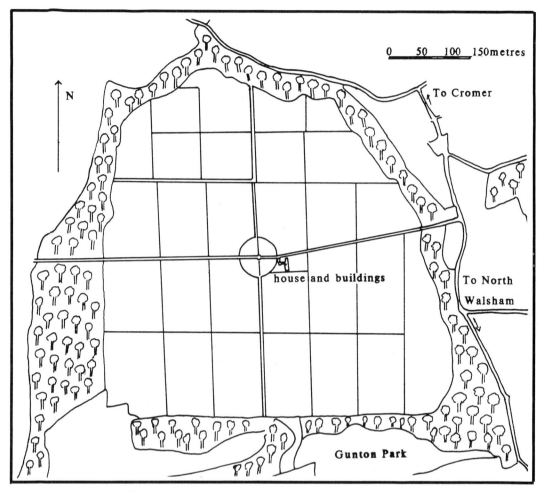

18. A plan of Tops Hill Farm at the north end of Gunton Park. Its layout, surrounded by a shelter belt and with a central circular plantation, was arranged specifically for the preservation of game.

3,000 acres in Breckland for sport. He lived in Henley-on-Thames and owned other sporting estates in Suffolk, Dumfries and Kirkcudbright. Lord Lothian, the absentee owner of Blickling, also cashed in on the vogue for shooting among the *nouveaux riches* and let the hall for the season for several years in the 1890s.

The other popular sport amongst the gentry was hunting and this, too, could be damaging to tenants' crops, while the preservation of foxes was a hazard to poultry. The master of the hounds was always a wealthy member of the gentry as he often took on much of the expense himself. Field sports, an interest in their parks and gardens and visiting their neighbours were the main leisure activities of the gentry, but the landowners had certain duties to perform for their tenants, the wider local community and the nation.

The gentry's first duty was towards their estates. They were not only responsible for the buildings on their farms and the condition of the cottages they owned; they felt it their duty to care for the general well-being of their tenants, also. The extent of this paternalism varied greatly from estate to estate, but often included school building and church restoration. The wives and daughters of the landlord might well visit the old and the sick, and perhaps even help in the local school. On the 5,000-acre estate of the Brampton Gurdons, Mrs. Gurdon and her daughters ran a Sunday School in Cranworth for those children who could not attend the daily schools and they were often to be seen in the village, 'engaged in errands of mercy'. Christmas was the time when landlord philanthropy was most in evidence and at Holkham three cattle were killed to provide meat for the poor. This tradition, along with other Christmas charities, was stopped for a year in 1847, because the parishioners were claiming them as a right. However they were soon resumed.

The buildings on an estate often reflect directly the concern felt by the landlord for improved farming. Most estates by the 19th century employed an estate manager. His job would be to run the office, sift requests from tenants and check that terms of leases were being kept and the land farmed well. Landlords also ran home farms which did more than provide fresh food for the house; it was hoped that they would set an example to the tenantry. The breeding of pedigree stock was a gentlemanly occupation. Lord Walsingham kept Suffolk ewes and rams which sold in Europe as well as Britain and his one-month old lambs were said to be worth £50 each. The most famous breeder in Norfolk was the Earl of Leicester. His stock was sold to farmers throughout Norfolk and elsewhere. His estates were undoubtedly the best managed in Norfolk throughout the 19th century. In spite of his political activities, Thomas William Coke had always taken a great interest in the running of his estates and he is remembered for the large sums he spent on farm buildings, some of which were built on a very grandiose scale. His annual sheep shearings were an advertisement for improved farming and were held from the end of the 18th century until 1821.

Another of the well-run estates of the early 19th century was that of Lord Suffield around Gunton Hall. Farms were laid out afresh and new premises built. 'His first concern was for his tenants. He built and endowed a handsome school at Thorpe, put all the farms and cottages into thorough repair, made roads, built a wharf on the canal at Antingham and erected a bone crushing mill that proved most profitable to the farmers.'

Not all estates were well managed. In 1861 the Duke of Norfolk (himself an absentee landlord) commissioned a report on the condition of his 11 Norfolk farms. The lack of landlord interest over the previous years is very apparent from the dilapidations described. The report pointed out that if the farm buildings were better, more able tenants might be attracted to the estate. 'The time has come when a considerable outlay must be made if this property is to be raised to a condition worthy of its hereditary owner.' Certainly the amount of landlord interest directly affected the standard of farm buildings and therefore of farming on an estate.

The running of the household was the responsibility of the lady of the house and it could prove to be an arduous task. After the death of Thomas William Coke's first wife, his elder daughter, Elizabeth, took on this duty when she came of age. She performed the role capably for many years, but after Coke's remarriage she was glad to hand over the responsibility and wrote to her future husband, John Stanhope, in 1822, 'She [Mrs.

19. & 20. Photograph and original elevations drawn by G. A. Dean in 1853 for the building of the home farm and estate workshops at Longlands, Holkham. These impressive buildings with their all-important clock tower were condemned as over-extravagant by many of the Earl of Leicester's contemporaries.

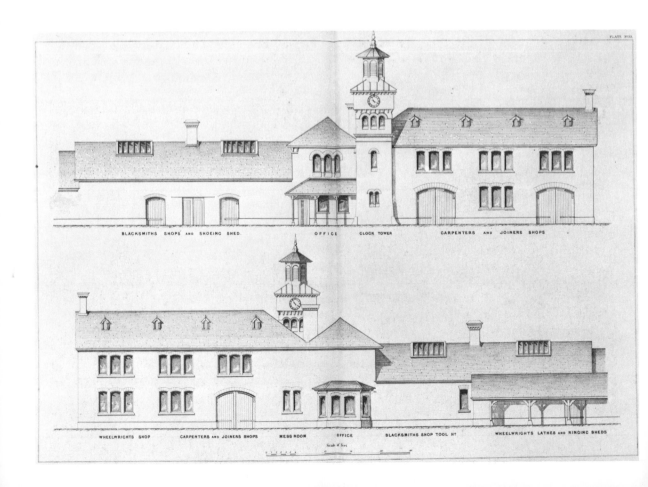

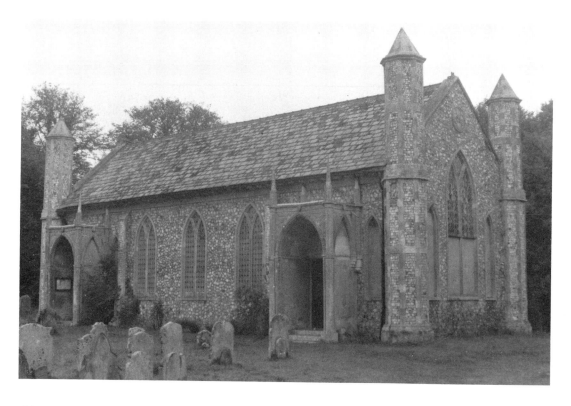

21. & 22. Thorpe Market school and church. Thorpe Market school is a huge and impressive building erected by Lord Suffield in 1826. The church was restored in the late 18th century, but the two porches were added in a similar style to those on the school, presumably at about the same date.

Coke] probably finds what I have found during several years, that this house entails a perpetual sacrifice of ones feelings and inclinations'. Between 30 and 40 servants were employed at Holkham and, when visitors came, they often brought their own servants with them, so the numbers were greatly increased. To feed this large establishment as many as 30 cattle and 400 wethers would be killed annually from the Home Farm.

The LeStrange family and their servants at Hunstanton consumed a sheep a week, but we do not know what other meat they ate. The cost of food for the Windhams and their 15 servants at Felbrigg Hall, a similar establishment about 20 miles east of Hunstanton along the north coast, in about 1850 is given below. Meat was the largest item, but the expense of imported foodstuffs such as spices, sugar, tea and coffee is also shown.

Beer – £200 p.a
Wine – £100 p.a.
Charcoal – £5 p.a.
Coal – £100 p.a.
Butcher's bills – £5 5s. per week
Bacon, ham, etc. – 7s. 6d. per week
Butter and eggs – 10s. per week
Breadcorn, flour, etc. – £1 10s. per week
Cheese – 4s. per week
Poultry – £1 per week
Poultry food – 5s. per week
Fish – 10s. per week
Spices and fruit – 15s. per week
Soap, candles, etc. – £1 per week
Tea, coffee, sugar – £1 1s. per week
Total – £1,115 p.a.

The total expenses at Felbrigg Hall amounted to just over £3,000 a year and included about £400 for coach horses and carriages, £448 for hunting horses and hacks, £440 for the hounds, £216 for cart horses and another £60 for other horses. Game preservation cost £210 and keeping the gardens in order another £310. Servants' wages were £147, their clothes £27. To live in the style of even the more modest gentry meant owning estates of 4-5,000 acres in the mid-19th century.

A duty which had been undertaken by the gentry since Elizabethan times had been the provision of the Justices of the Peace. In the 1880s there were well over 200 J.P.s in Norfolk drawn from the landowners and clergy. At the beginning of the century their duties were very wide, covering all aspects of riot control, provision for the poor, maintenance of roads and bridges, and the supervision of ale houses. During the 19th century the creation of the Poor Law Boards and, after 1888, County Councils, reduced their duties to purely legal ones, but many of the gentry became members of these new bodies, thus continuing their work in their traditional fields.

Rider Haggard was a member of the Board of Guardians for a short time as well as the first chairman of Ditchingham Parish Council. He was also a J.P. and his duties in 1898 included the licensing of public houses, the registering of lunatics, enforcing affiliation orders, coping with petty crime, the enforcement of school attendance and of vaccination, with the added complication of deciding whether objections were conscientious or not.

Only the most influential and wealthy amongst the local gentry could attempt to become directly involved in national politics. Huge fortunes were needed to fight elections. In 1768 the four candidates for the county seats probably spent over £40,000 between them while, at a later date, Thomas William Coke spent £20,000 (the equivalent of a year's rent from his land). Prospective M.P.s also needed 'county standing' and to achieve this they had to be from old county families whose names would be familiar to voters. There were only six parliaments between 1715 and 1796 when one of the members for Yarmouth was not a Townshend and five between 1702 and 1831 when one for Lynn was not a Walpole. In spite of these difficulties, there were always those with a thirst for power or a genuine desire to serve who wanted to compete for a seat in the House of Commons, valuing the honour that election brought.

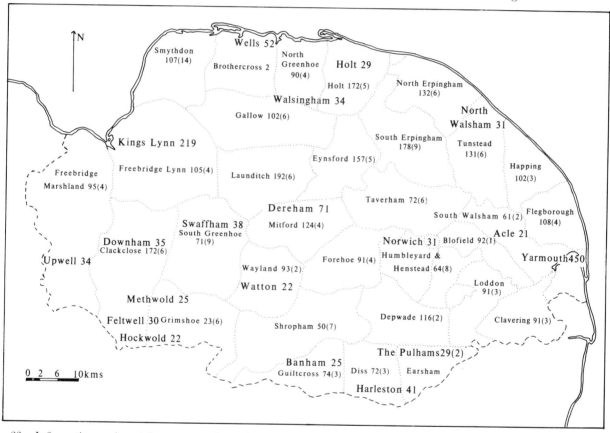

23. Information replotted from a map drawn by Humphry Repton for Thomas William Coke in 1786 showing 'the influence operating in the electors of Norfolk', to help him to plan his strategy for recapturing a county seat, lost four years previously. It shows the number of electors in each Hundred of Norfolk (the number for the larger villages and towns is given separately). The figure in brackets represents the number of prominent gentry with an income of over £1,000 a year and thus thought to influence no fewer than 20 voters. One hundred and ninety such territorial interests are plotted, an indication of the county's wealth and its potential for independence. This situation would have changed little until the widening of the franchise in 1832.

However, it would be wrong to think that the few local families with the greatest standing controlled local politics. Below them were the local gentry who had considerable influence over voters. One hundred and fifty of them are shown on Repton's political map drawn for Thomas William Coke at the end of the 18th century. These gentry would choose which candidate to support, not primarily because of his politics, but more because of family links and feelings of gratitude. Similarly, an intended or even unintended insult could lose a candidate the vote of a friend, and in turn, the votes of those he influenced. The lack of a letter asking for support at election time might be enough of a snub to change the political leanings of one man and his followers.

Up to the Parliamentary Reform Act of 1832, the County of Norfolk sent two M.P.s to Westminster, while the boroughs of Norwich, Yarmouth and Kings Lynn sent two more each. The two additional seats for the much smaller towns of Thetford and Castle Rising were controlled by the Duke of Grafton and Lord Petre, and the Walpole family respectively. There were about 5,000 40-shilling freeholders in Norfolk who were entitled to vote – about one-eighth of the county's adult male population. In Norwich, by 1831, there were 4,000 voters out of a total population of just over 61,000. In Yarmouth 1,700 of the 24,115 inhabitants could vote and in Kings Lynn, 3,000 out of 13,370.

Local families and their influence remained important after 1832. In some ways it increased as their £50-leaseholders gained the vote. On the Hare estate near Downham Market the owner was advised to increase the size of some of his smaller occupations to bring the tenants within the franchise and so consolidate his influence. In a reference for a prospective tenant on a neighbouring estate, the agent for Ketteringham wrote in 1848, 'I don't know whether you think of your tenants' politics, but Alden's family have always acted against us here.' Until the introduction of the secret ballot in 1872, voters were usually careful not to vote against the interests of their landlords, although too much interference could be resented. Clare Sewell Read's election victory in 1865 over Colonel Coke, the brother of the Earl of Leicester, was in part attributed to a revolt against landlord interference when Lord Leicester had issued an 'ill-advised and generally condemned circular to the tenantry on the subject of their votes'. As late as 1863, a local candidate felt that he should ask permission from the owner of Felbrigg before canvassing his tenantry.

Before the introduction of the payment of M.P.s in 1911 only those with private means could afford to sit at Westminster. Clare Sewell Read's election expenses in the 1870s were over £4,000. Only slowly did the situation change with industrialists such as J. J. Coleman and Sir E. H. Lacon holding seats in Norwich and North Norfolk by the 1880s.

Although the position of the gentry within rural society appeared to change very little during the 19th century, it did suffer several setbacks. With the establishment of local School Boards and Poor Law Boards as well as Parish and County Councils, landowners no longer controlled local affairs to the extent that they had previously. Successive parliamentary reform had weakened their control over political life and, by 1900, land was no longer the main source of wealth. Industry was far more profitable. The agricultural depression at the end of the century meant that rents fell dramatically. On the Holkham estate the income from rent in 1900 was less than half the level of 1870 and this sort of figure was typical of other areas. This decline in income meant that lifestyles had to be adapted accordingly. The great house was often locked up while its owners lived a simpler style of life elsewhere, perhaps letting their house for the shooting season. The Rolfe family of Heacham joined the many English gentlemen who had chosen to live in Naples because the cost of living was lower there. Sometimes it was almost impossible to let farms, so owners were forced to take them in hand. Rider Haggard was directly involved in the management of farms that had previously been tenanted. Some members of the family might well enter one of the professions or 'the City', while any spare cash was invested in stocks and shares rather than in the estate as agricultural prosperity declined. Improvement to farms would not increase the rent, but it might be necessary to keep tenants.

The prestige of land outlived its profitability. By 1900 land was an expensive luxury, but one for which many landlords were still prepared to pay.

Chapter Three
Farms and Farmers: Years of Prosperity and Progress

By the early years of the 19th century the last of the open fields and most of the commons had recently been enclosed and new thorn hedges were becoming established. A surplus of cheap labour ensured that hedges, old and new, were kept well trimmed and ditches cleaned. Buildings were in good order and fields carefully tended to produce heavy yields. Flocks of sheep were grazing on improved pasture or folded on turnips in the winter. Cattle spent the summer on the wetter meadows, which produced lush grass, and the winter in yards where the manure could easily be collected and then spread on the fields. Contrasting with this scene of order and prosperity were the labourers' cottages, many of which were ill-cared for, over-crowded and almost derelict. Farm buildings were far better looked after than the houses of those who worked in them.

On the heavy clay lands in the south of the county conditions were less good than those on the better soils. Here land was difficult to drain and the small owner-occupier farmers who were typical of this area could not afford to install anything better than the very impermanent bush drains which needed replacing every few years. While much of the arable was kept tidy and as free of weeds as a well tended garden, most of the permanent pasture was very different. These areas included common land, which was usually neglected, meadows in river valleys, the fens and the broads. 'In all parts of the county we find them overgrown by all sorts of spontaneous rubbish, bushes, briars and rushes; the water stagnant; ant hills numerous; in a word left in a state of nature by men who willingly make all sorts of exertions to render their arable land clean, rich and productive.' (1804)

The term 'farmer' included those with a few acres combining farming with some other village craft such as blacksmithing, and those with large sums of capital at their disposal working up to 1,000 acres. In between, the average farmer worked a smallholding with only his family to help him and only a small surplus for sale. He was often illiterate and it is surprising how many farmers around Suffield, for instance, paying rents of up to £50 at the end of the 18th century, were unable to sign the audit accounts and had to make their marks instead. Most diaries and accounts which were kept have been lost which makes the writing of the history of the typical 19th-century farmer an extremely difficult task.

The majority of Norfolk farms in 1850 were under 100 acres and a quarter were between 100 and 200 acres, so most farmers worked on a small scale with little capital, relying on the farm to produce the manure, seed and feed for their livestock. The developments of 'high farming' passed them by. The occupiers of the smallest holdings were often very poor indeed. The Rev. Armstrong, vicar of Dereham, describing the small farms around Shipdham in the 1850s, wrote, 'These little masters are often worse off than the labourers who work on small farms'.

Farmers with 100 acres could be comfortably off. John Garwood of Norton Subcourse, who died in 1830, probably farmed about this amount as his inventory lists five horses,

24. Digging bush drains at Bedingham Farm: an illustration from Rider Haggard's *A Farmer's Year* (1899).

which was the right number for a farm of this size. In his house there was a kitchen, parlour, four bedrooms and a servants' room. In his parlour, as well as tables, chairs and a bureau, he had two cupboards with glass-panelled doors containing glass and a tea service. The only implements he had were a plough, a hoe, harrows, carts and a waggon as well as riddles and a corn screen in the barn. There were harness and traces in the stable. A larger farm was that of John Lyall with nine horses, a bigger house and a wider range of implements; he owned a gig and other luxuries such as books and a barometer.

Amongst the farmers with more than 500 acres were the men who led the way in agricultural progress. John Hudson of Castle Acre was renowned for his 'high farming' methods in the middle years of the century. He was a founder member of the Royal Agricultural Society and a regular contributor to its journal. The Overman family at Weasenham and Burnham Sutton, and the Becks at Sussex farm, Burnham Market, were also in the forefront of improvement.

Landlords and their agents were always interested in watching the developing skills of the younger generation, assessing whether they would make good tenants if allowed to follow in their fathers' footsteps. The agent at Holkham would sometimes take a tenant's son with him on one of his tours of inspection so that the boy could learn from seeing other farms. Farmers would apply to landlords for advice in placing their sons. The agent at Ketteringham wrote in his diary after a discussion about the future of the son of a tenant, 'As to William, I thought he had better go as a bailiff or manager for a time to some good farmer – if he managed well, then something of a farm might be found for him.' When tenants wished to move from one estate to another, the future agent would seek a reference from the previous estate. One such reference was sought and received at Ketteringham in 1848. 'He and his father before him have occupied a small farm in Shelton for many years – a very respectable man with more intelligence than the majority of farmers.'

Up to the 1870s the tenant farmers formed a very tight community. They often remained on the same farm for several generations and their daughters married neighbouring farmers. However, as the agricultural depression began to bite this cosy situation, the dominance of old established families, well known in their locality, began to wane. Some of the old names disappeared and new men, often with capital made outside farming, came to take on the vacant farms.

25. Pettywell Farm near Reepham. This early 19th-century farm is typical of many. The substantial house may well be pre-19th century, but it has been given a Georgian facade, suggesting the increase in the social standing of its owner. The scattered farm buildings with a barn and cartlodge with a granary above in the foreground show no sign of the rationalisation so usual by the mid-19th century.

The county is very clearly divided into two areas, recognised by the agricultural journalist and Suffolk farmer, Arthur Young, as the 'wet' and the 'dry', or the areas of heavy and light soils. The light soils of the north-west were dominated by the great estates and their land was mostly divided into large farms of over 300 acres. To the south and east, however, where the land was much heavier, there were far more owner-occupiers, usually with smaller farms. Their numbers were declining during the second half of the 18th century. Nathaniel Kent, the writer and land agent who worked on many Norfolk estates, wrote, 'numerous little places of the yeomanry have fallen into the hands of men of fortune'. He was afraid that the decline of the small farmer would mean a shortage of the goods they traditionally produced, such as pigs, poultry and dairy produce.

By the beginning of the 19th century, Norfolk farming had already gone through at least one generation of change. Sheep, which had been so important in the Middle Ages and Tudor times, had been replaced by cereals as the most valuable crop. Increased output as a result of the enclosure of open fields and commons and the introduction of crop rotations where root crops and improved grasses did away with the need for the fallow year, had enabled grain production to increase to such an extent that, in spite of population expansion and the growth of towns, home prices remained low and so exports continued to be important. After 1760, when the population was rising at its fastest, exports began to decline and, although at the end of the 18th century Norfolk was exporting more grain than the rest of England put together, much of this was coastal traffic around to London. Some wealthy farmers had their own sloops at Wells, 'which were constantly employed in taking corn to London and bringing back rape cake manure from Holland, Hull or London, wherever it could be secured at the best and cheapest rate' (1804).

Improvements had begun in the good loams of north-east Norfolk where independently-minded owner-occupier farmers, seeking new sources of income with the decline in the value of wool, looked across the North Sea to the new crops being grown in Holland, and began copying them on their farms with very good results. There are numerous 18th-century examples of Norfolk farmers sending to Holland for turnip, clover and lucerne seed. Improvements had been going on for well over 100 years when William Marshall wrote in 1787, 'In east Norfolk alone we are to look for that regular and long established system of practice which has deservedly raised the name of Norfolk husbandmen'.

The owners of great estates soon realised the potential of these improvements on their lands. The drier chalky and sandy soils often required more capital before they could be improved and here was a situation where landlord and tenant worked together. Light soils needed heavy marling, sometimes as much as 80 loads an acre, and farm leases would stipulate how much marling the tenant was expected to do. Marl is a chalky subsoil which was spread on the fields to improve fertility. After the initial spreading, another 30 loads would be put on after 16 or 20 years. It was an expensive and time-consuming business and rent allowances were often made for the work involved.

Although this was generally to the tenants' benefit in the long run, there was one instance when it was not. In the very light Breckland soils where sheep farming had been the most profitable way of using the land, much marling was being carried out in the 1820s and '30s. This seemed to make the land unhealthy for sheep, and tenants were complaining that their lambs were dying at weaning of a disease they called 'warping'. This was put forward as a reason for not paying rents. Mr. Deforges, who rented 212 acres on the Walsingham estate around Stanford, 'has lost this season [1836] nearly 200 lambs being warped in consequence of claying land'. Sheep were themselves

26. A marl pit.

an important element in improving the soil. They were fed in the turnip fields and their manure was very highly prized, allowing the cultivation of cereals in areas previously considered too light.

The 19th century opened with Britain at war with France and twice, in 1797 and 1803-5, there was a threat of invasion. During most of the war, Napoleon was able to enforce a blockade, preventing Britain from trading with Europe. This led inevitably to food shortages and high prices for farmers. This in turn gave landlords the opportunity to raise rents. It was worth draining and improving land to get crops of cereals. Much of Breckland, described as 'a region of warrens and sheep walks, scattered with a scanty cultivation, yet highly improvable' (1807) was ploughed up for the first time. The lines of twisted fir trees which still cross the area were planted as windbreaks at this time. Commons were enclosed and marling begun, but cultivation was often unprofitable after the war ended and cereal prices dropped. It was not only in Breckland that enclosure and land improvement might prove uneconomic in peacetime conditions. The commons of the mid-Norfolk parish of Longham, enclosed in 1815, had comprised the least fertile land in the parish. In 1816 much work was still needed to bring the area under cultivation, but with the end of the war grain prices had dropped and John Hastings, described by his landlord's agent as 'a zealous and industrious tenant', was 'heartbroken by his present undertaking'.

The landlord's main contribution to improved farming was the provision of a well laid out enclosed farm with a good set of buildings; many farms on large estates were rebuilt at this time. Valuable cereal crops needed housing and threshing; for this large barns with several threshing floors were needed. These barns are monuments to the first agricultural revolution which can be seen throughout the county.

The increasing wealth of the farmers allowed their standard of living to rise. Often they continued to live in the rambling old manor houses of their ancestors, with wings for living-in farm servants, and servants' halls where all the farm workers were fed. Some landowners, foremost among them Coke of Holkham, felt that to attract the men of capital required to improve his farms he must provide prestigious houses. Fine late-Georgian residences, faced in fashionable yellow brick and often roofed in slate, were built all over the Holkham estate. As the social status of this wealthy group of tenants rose, they no longer wanted their farm labourers living in and moved them to farm cottages.

Improvements in farm layout, crop rotation and livestock breeding and husbandry are typical of the Napoleonic war period, but very little farm machinery was introduced. There was a surplus of labour in the countryside and so, with wages at starvation level, there was very little incentive to mechanise. If machines put men out of work, then the men and their families would have to be supported from the poor rate. William Marshall wrote in 1787, 'Notwithstanding the high degree of cultivation in which the

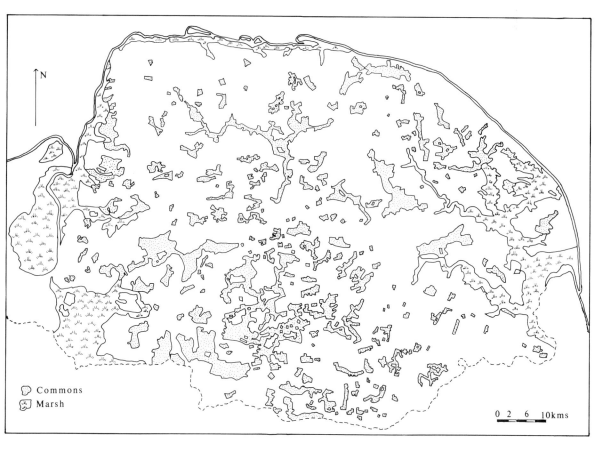

27. The commons in Norfolk at the time of Faden's map (1797). Although commons survived across the county, there are more in the south and Breckland than in the already improved north-west.

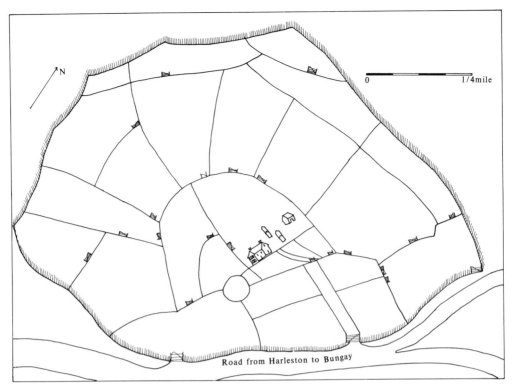

28. Earsham Hall farm is an example of a farm developed in the 18th century. Much of this irregular field layout centred on the house survives today although the 17th- and 18th-century buildings were replaced in the late 19th century. In 1804, Arthur Young described it as 'a fine farm, as compact as a table, without a footpath, near a town and a navigation with beautiful soils and situation'.

29. In contrast, these two farms on the Holkham estate were reorganised in the late 18th century. The fields are mostly rectangular, many containing marl pits. The stippled areas are permanent pasture.

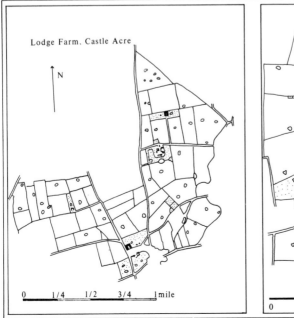

Lodge Farm, Castle Acre

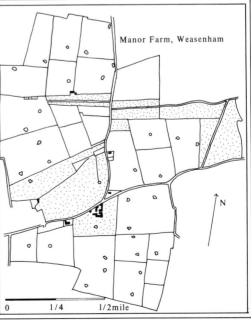

Manor Farm, Weasenham

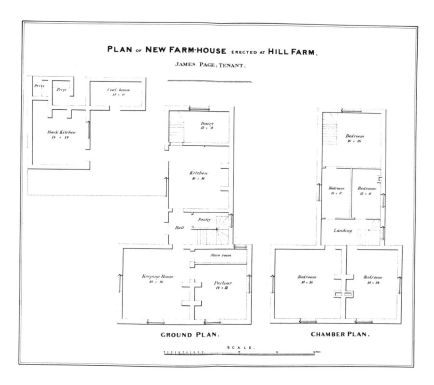

PLAN OF NEW FARM-HOUSE ERECTED AT HILL FARM.

JAMES PAGE, TENANT.

GROUND PLAN.   CHAMBER PLAN.

SCALE.

30.   These plans for the houses on newly created farms in the Fens near Downham Market belonging to the Hare estate show something of the social status of the tenant farmer. Both farms were large (just over 400 acres) and their houses show that tenants demanded certain standards. Both have back staircases leading to servants' rooms and separate parlours and keeping (dining) rooms as well as the kitchen. Both have dairies within the house. Newbridge Farm is the larger (487 acres) and so it is not surprising that the house is correspondingly more spacious.

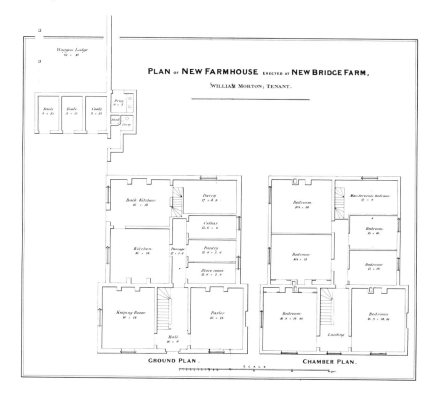

PLAN OF NEW FARMHOUSE ERECTED AT NEW BRIDGE FARM,

WILLIAM MORTON, TENANT.

GROUND PLAN.   CHAMBER PLAN.

SCALE.

31. Old farming methods survived on smallholdings and allotments into this century. This late 19th-century photograph from Hethersett shows the use of dibbles on a family plot.

lands of Norfolk are undoubtedly kept, no county has less variety of implements. There is not perhaps a drill, a horse hoe or scarcely a horse rake in Eastern Norfolk.' Writers such as Arthur Young claimed dibbled seed did better than broad-cast, but it required a lot of labour. A team of workers consisted of one man using two heavy iron dibbles and two women or children. A dibble was made of an iron rod with an egg-shaped knob on the end. The dibbler walked backwards dropping the dibbles into the newly-ploughed land, making two rows of holes. He would be followed by the two droppers who put about three seeds into each hole. This team would expect to seed about three-quarters of an acre a day. Although the seed drill was available from the 1780s, it was said to waste seed and so it was some time before prejudices were overcome and seed drills introduced. Many farmers were still dibbling some of their wheat in the 1840s.

The end of the Napoleonic Wars in 1815 brought a sudden decline in grain prices, but this did not last long and, although profits were never again as high as they had been in the years of wartime shortages, by 1830 they had picked up enough to keep all reasonable land in cultivation. Marginal land such as the light soils of Breckland was abandoned and soon reverted to heath, with rabbits once again the most important product.

Decline in profits meant that rents could not always be paid but on many estates investment on farm improvements continued at a high level to keep old tenants and attract new ones. On the Holkham estate at least six of the 70 farms were undergoing major improvements in any one year between 1815 and 1830. In a few years in the 1820s as much as £15,000 was spent by Lord Suffield on improvements on his 8,000-acre estate in north-east Norfolk. Mr. Wright, a Norwich land agent, pointed out in 1833, 'If there were a farm let in bad condition, it would not let so readily as it used to, as tenants are more cautious in expanding and do not like to lay out capital on an uncertain speculation'. The price of grain reached its lowest in 1833 at 28 shillings a quarter in Norwich market (in contrast to 130 shillings a quarter in 1806), yet the land on the whole remained well cultivated and well stocked. After this date prices remained over 50 shillings a quarter until the 1870s. Farmers weathered these bad years because there was an increased emphasis on cattle rearing. Cattle numbers trebled between 1815 and 1843. Whilst the value of grain remained steady, that of cattle was rising and so a mixed system of agriculture was the most profitable.

32. Very few stationary steam engines were used on Norfolk farms and this barn near Narborough is unusual in that there is a chimney, possibly indicating that a steam engine was installed there.

Agricultural development in the first half of the 19th century was dominated by Thomas William Coke, later Earl of Leicester, but known to his contemporaries as 'Coke of Norfolk'. Although legends about his work for agriculture, some of which have since been proved to be inaccurate, gathered around his name, he certainly did make an important contribution. On his estates he continued the tradition of farm improvement, thus attracting good tenants with money to finance intensive farming. He

33. A threshing team with tackle owned by Stephen Dann of North Tuddenham working on a local farm in 1912.

continued to grant long leases which encouraged the occupiers to think that it was worthwhile improving the land, and these leases often included husbandry clauses enforcing crop rotations on the estate. He promoted the introduction of new livestock breeds such as Devon cattle and Leicester and Southdown sheep. Perhaps more important, he ran an annual sheep shearing from the 1770s until the 1820s. This event, held at sheep shearing time in early July, began as an annual gathering of local farmers to exchange ideas, inspect the sheep and visit the home farm. They soon grew into a great national three-day event and gave Holkham and its owner much publicity. One enthusiastic visitor claimed that the sheep shearings 'had indeed changed the habits and conditions of agricultural society'.

For such an event, which included visits to local tenant farms as well as the home farm within the park, Coke needed to have gathered together an intelligent, progressive and wealthy tenantry and these men, as much as their landlord, were responsible for the fame of north-west Norfolk in the early 19th century. Although the sheep shearings ended in 1821, Coke continued to be in the forefront of agricultural improvement until he died in 1842. A monument erected in Holkham park shows some of the things that made him famous. Reliefs represent the sheep shearings, the granting of a lease and the creation of an irrigation scheme, while a Devon bull, a Southdown sheep, a seed drill and a plough are represented on the corners of the base. It is perhaps significant that not only Coke, but also some of his tenants and friends who helped make Holkham famous, are shown on this monument to agricultural progress.

By the 1840s, farming was again prosperous and was entering the period of high farming which characterised the mid-19th century. Innovation continued, but it was a different type of change from that made earlier.

Firstly there were developments in machinery. These had been held up because of the lack of demand from farmers while labour was abundant and cheap. From 1850 however, the population of most villages was beginning to decline and agricultural wages to rise, so that there was more interest in labour-saving machines from the farmers themselves. Previously there had been steam- and horse-powered threshing machines, but attempts to install them often led to riots by men afraid of losing winter work. Machine breaking was a problem of the early 1830s, when not only threshing machines but a new saw mill at Gunton became targets. The problem of a surplus labour force is vividly illustrated in a description of a farm at Costessey where a threshing machine was used, but powered by men rather than horses, 'which costs as much as to flail – we are too many men so I do not use horse-power'. On many farms in the 1840s some of the crop was still flailed by hand, especially in the winter when there was little alternative employment. Very few stationary steam engines were erected because of the expense of transporting coal. Of more significance was the availability after 1850 of portable steam engines which could be taken with the threshing tackle to the stack. The costs of carting could be much reduced if the corn was threshed in the field. Gradually the barn lost its importance as the centre of the farm where the grain was stored and threshed, and these great, often cathedral-like structures became obsolete, used for little more than implement and feed stores. Sometimes the great double doors were blocked up on one side and removed on the yard side so that the barn became a shelter shed for cattle: a practice frowned upon by agents because if the cattle were horned it could be very injurious to the building.

34. A team of mowers in a harvest field at Weybourne in the 1850s.

35. The harvest team and the completed stacks on Vale Farm near Stibbard in 1900.

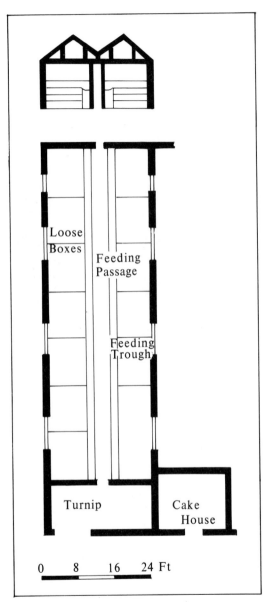

36. Plan of loose boxes at West Lexham, erected in 1850, showing the central feeding passage, troughs and individual stalls.

The introduction of machinery into the harvest field did not take place until after 1850, although by that date most Norfolk farmers mowed their crop with scythes rather than reaping with sickles. The variety of tasks involved in mowing, binding and shocking up the sheaves, as well as raking up what had been missed, meant that the corn field at harvest time was crowded with women and children as well as men. Gradually the introduction of the mechanical reaper, and then the reaper-binder, reduced the size of the harvest team.

The 1850s saw not only advances in the development of machinery, but also in agricultural science. The need for the four-course system was challenged as new chemical fertilisers made it possible to grow corn crops in succession without reducing the fertility of the soil. By the 1860s farmers on the large estates were seeking permission to depart from the terms of their leases to grow more grain. On most estates this permission was granted. As the value of livestock products rose, more intensive methods were used here as well. Imported cattle cake became an added expense for farmers and better livestock accommodation was needed. Cattle yards were improved and many were subdivided to allow for the closer supervision of stock and the regulation of how much they ate. On the more progressive farms, loose boxes were built for the individual feeding of cattle. The most advanced type of cattle accommodation, developed by the 1850s, was the covered yard, used in conjunction with loose boxes. Young stock would be kept under cover rather than in open yards both to keep them warmer and to conserve manure. They were then finally fattened for market in the loose boxes. Few farmers were prepared to go to the very considerable expense of putting up covered yards and very few were built. In Norfolk they are only found on the home farms of a few progressive estates.

The building of the railway meant that stock no longer had to walk to market. It had taken several days to walk sheep to Smithfield. Sheep lost an average of seven pounds on

37. These covered yards on a farm near Dereham were probably built for the home farm of an estate in about 1850. The cast-iron ventilation gratings are a characteristic feature of this particular estate.

the way and bullocks 28 pounds. As a result of the opening of the railway, between one-third and one-half of the cattle sold at Smithfield had been fattened in Norfolk.

The advocates of 'high farming' were spending £2,000-£3,000 a year on animal feeds and £1,000 on fertilisers to farm 1,000 acres on which 150 steers and 2,500 sheep might be kept. Optimists believed that nothing could hold back agricultural science, whose main aim was the expansion of production. Increased output at almost any cost was thought to be worthwhile as, with an expanding population, the domestic market for food was insatiable.

High farming did have its critics. Clare Sewell Read farmed 800 acres at Honingham Thorpe and in 1865 he became the first tenant farmer M.P. and the farmers' advocate in the House of Commons. In 1858 he had written that a quarter more wheat was grown in Norfolk than 15 years previously yet he feared that the supply of cheap grain from the New World was bound to increase and was worried about the diminishing returns on investments which at the moment were still profitable. He denounced science as a two-edged sword. New machinery saved time and labour, not money. He was doubtful about the value of artificial fertilisers which were easily swept away by rain and did not restore the soil structure as farmyard manure did.

These advances in both livestock and cereal farming relied on the farmer being able to afford the high cost of purchased inputs such as fertiliser and animal feed; this sort of intensive farming was only profitable in times of high prices. Many farmers on smaller holdings with less capital continued to use rotations, to rely mainly on animal manure to keep their soil fertile, and to feed root crops to their stock.

The state of farming mid-century can be seen in the agricultural statistics collected by Poor Law Unions in 1854. The breakdown of figures union by union makes it possible to compare the proportions of crops grown across the county. Breckland stands out in great contrast to the rest. While elsewhere a mixed system predominated with grain accounting for between one-third and one-half of the acreage, in the infertile Thetford union only 6.35 per cent of the land was under cereal crops and a very high percentage of this was rye. In contrast, in the newly reclaimed fenland areas nearly half of the land (45.6 per cent) was growing cereals.

Turnips still dominated the root crops, although by 1850 mangolds were generally recognised as having a higher food value and to have a greater resistance to finger and toe disease (club root). Permanent pasture was most important in Broadland and parts of the Fens, where drainage for arable had not yet taken place. When William Marshall visited the Broads in the 1780s, he found much of the area under water in the winter. As a result of enclosures and the setting up of local drainage boards, windpumps were erected and by 1850 a transformation had taken place. Once useless marshland had become productive and much sought-after summer grazing.

The years of high prices and agricultural boom lasted until the 1870s and the area of land under crops rose steadily throughout the period. There were 1,005,135 acres in cultivation in Norfolk in 1854 and 1,086,767 by 1882. However, the proportion o different crops did change. The acreage of wheat declined while that of barley grew; ai indication that Norfolk was already specialising in the crop to which the soil ani climate was most suited. Turnips also declined after 1854 and were replaced by th more nutritious mangolds. In spite of sporadic outbreaks of foot and mouth disease, th number of cattle increased after 1854 and the prosperity of the countryside based on mixed farming system seemed set to continue.

Chapter Four
Farms and Farmers: Depression and Diversification

In the 1870s, C. S. Read's prophecy that cheap grain imports would render high farming unprofitable proved to be true. The price of grain in Norwich fell from about 65 shillings a quarter in 1872 to below 55 shillings for the rest of the century, reaching its lowest in 1894 at 25 shillings. Farmers were slow to understand the real cause of the problem. Many blamed the weather and certainly there were several poor years in the last quarter of the 19th century; 1879 was a particularly bad one. In the spring and early summer of 1885 there was a prolonged drought followed by heavy rain at harvest. Lord Lothian's agent at Blickling wrote, 'The present state of things is very disastrous and the future is most gloomy'.

The years 1891-2 were again cold and wet while 1893 brought drought which resulted in a poor wheat and barley harvest. The crop of hay was down by a third and only half of the normal turnip crop was lifted.

Decline in grain prices meant a decline in the amount of fertiliser used and farmers were more fussy about what they bought, only wishing to deal with reputable chemical companies such as Fisons at Thetford. Smaller family businesses such as that at the bone mills at Antingham, built with such optimism by the 3rd Baron Suffield in the 1820s, could no longer be let in the 1890s. It was not only cereals that suffered. There were also years of cattle disease. In 1885 cattle plague hit many herds and a mutual assurance association was set up for protection against loss. Liver fluke was also a recurring problem amongst sheep.

38. Clare Sewell Read as an old man.

43

39. David Scarfe, a shepherd on a farm near Weasenham, *c.*1900.

40. Robert Carver in front of his hut at Saham Toney, *c.*1900. At lambing time the shepherd lived in his hut in the fields with the ewes. The hurdle woven with straw leaning against the hut would have been used to provide the side of a wind-proof pen for a ewe and her new-born lamb.

41. Sheep dipping by contract sheep dippers from Wrenningham in the early 20th century. The sheep had to be lifted into the dip, but walked out on the far side where they stood in the elevated section while some of the dip drained back into the bath.

After disease and the weather, farmers blamed high wages. Farm wages had been rising and labourers were now in a stronger position to demand more as rural populations were declining. One large farmer claimed that the cost of labour had gone up by five shillings an acre between 1872 and 1881 and that the main increase in farming costs was the labour bill. All farmers were bitterly opposed to the unions and some blamed increased education both for reducing the number of boys available for work and equipping children for something better than fieldwork. C. S. Read complained that all the brightest and most intelligent labour had left the land.

Although C. S. Read supported the complaints about the price of labour, he was one of the few farmers who understood the real cause of the agricultural depression. He saw the future of British farming less in the provision of the traditional staples, wheat and barley, and more in catering for a new diversity of needs. Rising standards for those living in the towns and the availability of railway transport created a new market for fruit, vegetables and dairy produce. He travelled to North America in 1880 for The Royal Commission on Agriculture to look into the production of wheat there and its export to Europe, and he came back even more convinced of the need for British agriculture to diversify.

MANOR FARM,
LYNG,

4¼ Miles from Reepham, 2 Miles from Lenwade, on the Eastern and Midlands Railway, and 7 from Dereham.

AGRICULTURAL SALE OF
13 HORSES,

COMPRISING

9 Active CART MARES and GELDINGS, BAY ENTIRE CART STALLION, "CHARLIE," 3 PONIE S.

24 Head of NEAT STOCK,

CONSISTING OF

A DAIRY of 4 HOMEBRED and 2 SHORTHORN COWS, 5 SHORTHORN GRAZING STEERS and HEIFERS, 9 WEANLINGS, 8 CALVES, and ROAN SHORTHORN BULL,

WHITE SOW and 161 HEAD of FOWLS

WHICH

SALTER & SIMPSON

Are instructed to SELL BY AUCTION, without reserve,

On MONDAY, SEPTEMBER 26th, 1887,

TOGETHER WITH THE ASSORTMENT OF

AGRICULTURAL CARRIAGES, IMPLEMENTS, HARNESS, &c.,

The Entire HOUSEHOLD FURNITURE,

PLATE, LINEN, DAIRY UTENSILS, and other Effects,

Late the Property of Mrs. HANNAH COBON, Deceased.

Sale to Commence at 10.15. with the Furniture.

Luncheon at 1.30 o'clock.

42. Title page of a sales catalogue for the live and dead stock at Manor Farm Lyng in 1887. As farmers were giving up and sons not taking over on the death of their parents, farm sales became more frequent.

The price of grain dropped before that of livestock and so arable farmers were the first to be affected, but, by the 1890s, stock farmers were also suffering. The price of wool was declining from 1864 as a result of Australian and New Zealand imports. Later, refrigerated ships allowed frozen meat to be imported. However, the quality of this meat was never as high as the home-killed product, so the demand for British meat did not drop as fast as that for wheat. Norfolk malting barley still fetched good prices although it was no longer malted on farms. With the building of the railways, maltings became concentrated in the towns and farm maltings fell into disuse. One continued at Antingham Hall into the 1890s, but the land agent did not recommend the spending of too much on repairs: 'Would these malthouses be required by any other tenant? I should say no as country malt houses in the present day are of very little use or profit'.

To meet the new circumstances, farmers adapted their system to the production of high grade barley for sale to town maltings, and animals were kept less intensively on semi-permanent pasture. Farmers on the light soils were giving up the four-course rotation and instead laying down grass for sheep for five or six years, thus reducing the cost of tillage and labour. After 1881, the total cultivated area began to decline while the amount of pasture increased in the last quarter of the century from 214,479 to 288,510 acres.

One effect of the agricultural depression was that, for the first time, farms could not be relet and sometimes remained vacant or had to be taken in hand by the landlord. Families that had farmed for generations left and were replaced by newcomers, often from Scotland, where banks were prepared to lend money at more reasonable rates.

Many of these Scottish families are still in Norfolk. Twenty-eight of the 70 farms on the Holkham estates changed hands, many of them more than once, between 1880 and 1900. Most leases were now yearly ones as tenants did not want to commit themselves for any length of time. Rider Haggard described the changes that were taking place in the attitudes of tenant farmers in the 1890s. He did not regard the new tenants as proper farmers; 'It cannot be called farming, for without capital, without sufficient stock, without insight and determination to make this spot a home for years and by skill and adaptability to force the land to yield a living, how can a man farm in such times as these? He had better give it up and take to tax-collecting, after the shrewd example of a tenant of mine.'

One real chance for the tenant to air his grievances was at the annual audit, when the rent was paid and usually a dinner was given. The dinner served at Blickling was 'plain and substantial; roast and boiled beef and mutton, plum pudding . . . and a somewhat vigourous attack is made on the wine cellar.'

Rider Haggard describes one such occasion near his estate at Ditchingham, which was held in an hotel in the market town. The tenants would begin to arrive at midday to pay their rent, or more often, to explain why they could not. 'Also in these times he generally takes the opportunity to point out that a further reduction is absolutely necessary to enable him to live.' He then went on to describe the various types of tenant. 'There is the specious and horsey young man with a glib tongue, from which flow innumerable reasons why he should not pay his just debts.' At the other end of the scale is 'the silver-haired old gentleman who has been a tenant of the estate for 50 years and in all that time has never failed to meet his rent.' Most of the rents were paid by three o'clock and then 'everybody adjourned to a long old-fashioned room. Here the landlord takes the head of the table and the agent the foot, while the tenants range themselves in solemn lines on either side . . . the menu never varies from year to year.' After the drinking of the health of the Queen and of the landlord, came the landlord's speech.

> How well the tenant knows that speech! It begins invariably with a solemn wail or lament over the shocking bad times, which as a general rule he is bound to confess are even worse than they were at the last gathering. Then, while his audience shake their heads and sigh, he rises to a more cheerful note and talks of the inherent pluck and nobility of the character of Englishmen which . . . enable them . . . to put up the price of corn – how he will not specify. Then he gives some account of the farming of whatever country he may have just visited, America or Iceland or Egypt or the Hebrides or Mexico. This is generally the most popular part of his speech as there is a slight novelty about it.

The occasion ended with songs and the smoking of long clay pipes.

However, the cameraderie of these events could not for long blind the farmers to the long-term problems at the end of the century. The prosperity of earlier years had been replaced by pessimism and this could be seen in the state of farms. The cost and scarcity of labour was the excuse given for uncut hedges and clogged ditches. There was much more rough pasture and less care was taken of crops. The only growth sectors were horticulture, and dairying where the arrival of the Scottish farmers with their Ayrshire cows coupled with the increase in the railway network resulted in an expansion of output. By the end of the 19th century soft fruit was being grown in the Fens and the Broads but the main period of growth was after the First World War.

Only essential maintenance was carried out on buildings although sometimes an incoming tenant would demand improved livestock accommodation before he would

43. Strawberry pickers at Hethersett, *c.*1900. Market gardening, particularly near large centres of population, could prove a profitable alternative to a cereal crop.

44. Although there were very few innovations in farm machinery during the depression years, steam ploughing became more popular, particularly on very heavy land.

take the farm and so some new building did take place. Agents tried to persuade landlords to keep buildings in order in spite of bad times. Lord Suffield, for instance, was urged to 'improve with an eye to the future'.

In spite of the shifts in production and the reductions in profits in the last years of the 19th century, much of the life of the farm continued very much as before. Most farmers were growing slightly less grain, leaving fields under grass longer and perhaps trying a few acres of fruit and vegetables, whilst cutting back on maintenance work. The new century, however, was to bring about much more fundamental changes. The greatest adjustments in the agricultural scene were yet to come.

Chapter Five
Village Life

Even as late as 1901, agriculture was the largest single source of employment in Britain and until 1850 half the population was rural. This was particularly so in a county such as Norfolk, but it is difficult to piece together a clear picture of rural society and living conditions. In the early 19th century most countryfolk could not write and so they left few descriptions of their life and work. The information we have was mostly compiled by outsiders. These, particularly the artist and poet, give us a picture of rural contentment in the pastoral tradition while, at the other extreme, social reformers stressed the poverty and squalor of the agricultural labourers' lot.

45. The village tailor was a rare survivor into the early 20th century. However, this master tailor, W. A. Corbyn, still had one young apprentice, his son Stanley.

What is certain is that the 19th century brought many changes both to village and villagers. For instance, the early 19th-century village contained a great variety of craftsmen. Although agriculture was a very important employer, it was by no means the only one. Gradually, however, the number of crafts practised declined. Jessopp

46. Village brick kilns often survived into this century. The workers at Ludkins Brickyard in Banham were photographed in about 1900. The workforce included women and children as well as men.

47. Hethersett General Store, *c*.1900.

blamed this on the abolition of the turnpikes in the middle of the century, which enabled town tradesmen to send out their carts to the villages. This could well have been true in his own village of Scarning on the turnpiked Norwich to Kings Lynn road only a few miles from Dereham. In 1851 Scarning's population of 640 was served by a carpenter, two tailors, two shoemakers, two shops, a butcher, a wheelwright and a surgeon. By 1880 the tailors had disappeared and only one shoemaker and a shop remained, although the population was about the same. A newcomer was a 'cooper, basket and sieve maker', a type of craftsman familiar in many small communities up to 1914. Other typical craftsmen included blacksmiths, thatchers, hurdle makers and brick and tile makers. Although all these craftsmen might well turn to agricultural work if trade was slack or when extra labour was needed at harvest, they were usually better off than the agricultural labourers themselves. In a large village such as Foulsham as much as half the working population would be tradesmen and craftsmen. Frequently boys and girls would start off working in the fields, but later take up a craft. Census returns show how, very often, the head of the household was not an agricultural labourer, while his children were, and even the craftsmen would feel the pinch if the harvest was bad. Farmers would cut down on repairs and maintenance while agricultural wages would be cut.

By the end of the 19th century, the remoteness and the self-sufficiency of the villages were being broken down by the arrival of the railways. People were more likely to buy items such as hats and clothes from the market towns, although shoe making survived as a village craft for longer. Blacksmiths, harness makers and wheelwrights remained until the demise of the working horse, and many village shops until the arrival of cars and buses.

Families whose only source of income was agriculture were the worst off but their lot did improve during the 19th century, particularly in the last 40 years. Augustus Jessopp noticed a great improvement between 1860 and 1880. Wages were higher, children were better dressed and there was less female labour. Pictures and china ornaments had appeared in houses. 'Debt was no longer as universal as it was.'

Farmers had become more prosperous at the start of the 19th century, but their profits were not passed on to farm labourers and so the gulf between the farmer and those who worked for him grew. The demand for more grain meant that the acreage under cultivation was increased and more land was enclosed. Again it was the large farmers who benefited. Those who had previously been able to keep a few animals on the common and collect fuel there lost these rights and became entirely reliant on their wages for survival.

As the size of farms grew, the farmer needed more labour and, as he became more prosperous, he became more distant from his labourers. Weekly, daily or even hourly wages replaced yearly hire and living-in. This coincided with a period of great population increase at the end of the 18th century. The bargaining power of labour, particularly in an area such as Norfolk where alternative employment in industry was declining, was becoming weaker. Wages fell, often to starvation levels and cottage conditions were very poor indeed. A Norfolk farmer dated the decline in living-in from 1801 when corn prices were at their highest, although in fact it had been falling for the half century before. 'You cease to feed your men when it is hardest for them to feed themselves. People do not want the trouble of it and I believe this is the truth.'

48, 49 & 50. Three portraits of labourers in Weybourne taken shortly before 1856 by W. J. J. Balding as part of a photographic survey of all the inhabitants holding, where appropriate, the tools of their trade. The smock worn by the young man (*above left*) suggests that he may well have been a fisherman, and plate 49 (*above right*) shows Bob Lynes, the grave digger.

Although there were those who looked back nostalgically to the days of living-in labour, conditions had often been very poor. A 14-year-old boy could expect his board, but no wages, and the farmers were sometimes very brutal to their younger workers. Flogging and whipping was common and even expected of a respected farmer. Life generally was more brutal at that time. In the 1880s Rev. Jessopp visited old people in his parish and questioned them about their early days up to 70 years previously. The cruelties of living-in were described to him and this violence was reflected in home life. Fathers were remembered as hard and cruel, frequently flogging their children. Mothers were remembered with more affection; generally 'folks didn't take as much notice o'children as they do now.'

One effect of the enclosure of the commons was the end of fuel gathering there by the poor. Until the building of the railways, coal was very expensive in the countryside and there was a very real fuel shortage. Old Sally Tuttle, who was over 80 years of age, told Augustus Jessopp, 'I never saw coal till after I was married and I never burnt any till my second husband bade me bring some from Dereham. We used to bring it tied in a bundle and carry it on our heads.' Dereham was two or three miles from Scarning.

Over population led to low wages and Nathaniel Kent in his survey of Norfolk agriculture at the end of the 18th century said it was impossible to live on them. Many otherwise law abiding men resorted to poaching. Rural unemployment was up to about one-eighth of the labouring population, but a government committee of 1831 claimed that it was not 'beyond what the cultivation of the soil might fairly be said to require' because of the seasonal demand for labour. This callous attitude led to men accepting wages averaging between eight and nine shillings a week, which in years of bad harvests and high prices was below subsistence level.

Rather than raise wages, farmers preferred labourers to claim a dole from the parish to bring their income up to subsistence level, but this in turn raised the Poor Rate. The 17th-century Settlement Laws meant that a labourer was not eligible for poor relief outside his own parish, so it was often very difficult for him to move in search of work. The absurdity of this situation encouraged rate payers in some areas to look for an alternative method of helping the poor that removed the possibility of supplementary doles and so reduced the Poor Rate. The answer was found in the establishment of 'Houses of Industry' for groups of parishes which, after the passing of Gilbert's Act in 1782, could legally form themselves into 'corporations' to build 'workhouses'. By 1800 they had been built at Heckingham, Gressenhall (now the Norfolk Rural Life Museum), Wicklewood, Smallborough and Rollesby. They are found in the more densely populated central and east Norfolk parishes rather than the west and south.

There were no general rules governing the administration of Houses of Industry, but once they were built there was little help available for the poor unless they were willing to move into them and every effort was made to organise the inmates into productive employment. Many ran their own farms. At Gressenhall the 50-acre farm had ten dairy cows and also a windmill that ground flour for both the workhouse and for local farmers. The women and children spun and their work was sold to the weavers in Norwich. The plan of Smallburgh shows twine spinning rooms, a sack factory and a mill powered by a 'labour wheel'. Sacks were also made at Rollesby and spinning wheels were to be found in the small town workhouse in Swaffham. A very unusual

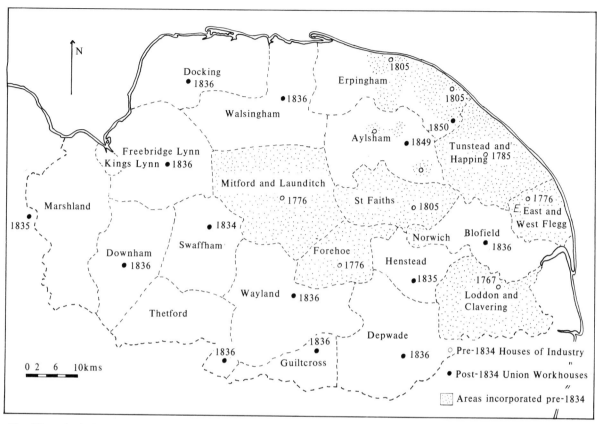

51. The stippled area on this map shows the parishes served by a House of Industry before 1834. The distribution pattern suggests that east and central Norfolk were the most pauperised and those areas dominated by the great estates in the north-west seem to have escaped incorporation, as have the areas of small owner-occupier farms in the heavy claylands to the south. The dashed lines show the boundaries of the Poor Law Unions set up in 1834.

system at Gressenhall workhouse allowed men to receive wages and keep a penny of every shilling they earned.

Whether the existence of Houses of Industry forced farmers to pay a living wage is not clear. Certainly labourers were living very near starvation levels throughout the Napoleonic Wars and after. Suffering the effects of inflation, long periods of unemployment, the decline in domestic industry and often denied the opportunity to work elsewhere, the labourer could hardly have been in a worse condition. An improvement might have been expected after the end of the war in 1815, when cheaper wheat from the continent might have been available in England. A glut of imported wheat forcing down the price of the home supply was just what the farmers feared and so the landowner-dominated parliament passed the Corn Laws which prevented the importation of grain until the price of English wheat reached 80 shillings a quarter. As a result, food riots spread through Norfolk and Cambridgeshire in 1816. Often led by shoemakers who were frequently the radical leaders in rural society, they were supported by the starving and frustrated labourers who attacked the corn millers as well as the farmers in their attempts to seize food and demand higher wages (usually two shillings a day). The riots resulted in two executions at Norwich Castle on 31 August 1816. In spite of the Corn Laws, the price of wheat remained depressed throughout the 1820s and wages fell to eight shillings a week. After 1826 the average weekly wage was hardly ever under 10 shillings but the danger of rick burning and machine breaking was never far away.

52. This photograph, illustrating an essay written by Augustus Jessopp, was published in *Arcady, for better or worse* in 1887. Jessopp wanted to show that the fashionable myths about the charms of rural life were very far from the truth.

In 1830 discontent again surfaced, this time in a series of riots known as the 'Swing' riots because the machine breaking and arson was often preceded by a threatening letter signed by 'Captain Swing'. As previously, the labourers were demanding wage increases and the removal of threshing machines. That the labourers had gained a certain amount of public support is shown by the fact that the magistrates of Tunstead and Happing made the surprising move of issuing a public notice asking farmers to stop using threshing machines and to pay 10 shillings a week. Workhouses were also a target for attack because they restricted the amount of poor relief men could get in their own homes. Those at Smallborough, Forncett and Attleborough were damaged. In some riots the farmers joined forces with the labourers and they all went to the parsons to demand a reduction in tithes. In such cases farmers made wage increases conditional on the reduction of tithes.

Although the Swing riots were over by the end of the year, feelings between farmer and labourer remained tense, and associations of farmers were established for the prevention of arson. A Norfolk witness to a Select Committee in 1833 claimed that the situation was so unpleasant that it deterred newcomers from

Key

1. Porter
2. Receiving wards
3. Infants' dayroom
4. Infants' yard
5. Boys' yard
6. Old men's dayroom
7. Industrial training rooms
8. Boys' dormitory
9. Old men's yard
10. Men's dayroom
11. Women's and infants' room
12. Women's yard
13. Girls' dayroom
14. Girls' yard
15. Garden
16. Dining Hall
17. Able-bodied women's
    dayroom
18. Kitchen

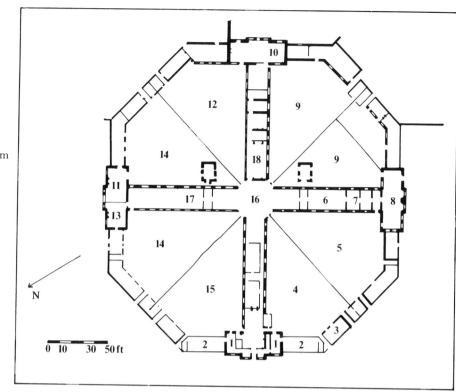

53. Plan of Pulham Market workhouse, 1836.

54. The main entrance to Aylsham Union Workhouse, erected in 1849 and designed as a humble reflection of the architecture of Blickling Hall.

becoming farmers. The struggle of 'keeping up profits by beating down wages is so painful that men are indisposed to embark on it'. Also, there was 'the nuisance of having a quantity of unemployed people teasing them for allowances and threatening them'. To the question, 'Is there the same good feeling between farmers and the labourers that there was formerly?', the answer was, 'Nothing like there was before the fires'.

Although workhouses had been introduced into Norfolk to end the allowance system of subsidising labour and so to reduce poor rates, allowances to make up wages had crept back during the years of agricultural depression when farmers claimed they could not afford to pay a living wage. In 1834, however, the system of poor relief was finally reformed nationwide by the passing of the Poor Law Amendment Act. Even though Norfolk already had many workhouses, a certain amount of reorganisation was needed to bring the county in line with the requirements of the new Poor Law. Some of the corporation workhouses were too small and unsuitable for serving any of the 18 Poor Law Unions into which the county was divided. Twelve new workhouses were built and others such as Gressenhall were enlarged. Central control was administered by the Poor Law Board in London which laid down strict rules on how workhouses should be run. Even the design of the buildings was controlled from London. Inmates were divided by age and sex which resulted in one of the most hated aspects of the system – the break up of families. This led to riots at Rollesby in 1836 when part of the workhouse was burnt down. Because workhouse work was now to be unpleasant and monotonous, workhouse farms were given up and land sold. Food was also to be 'so regulated as in no case to exceed in quantity or quality the ordinary diet of any class of able-bodied labourers living in the same district'. However, people who entered the workhouse were sure of regular, if unvaried, meals and children received some sort of education which was usually not available outside. Although the central Poor Law Office had issued standard plans, most Norfolk unions chose to employ their own architect which led to a slight variation in style in efforts to produce suitably prestigious buildings such as that at Aylsham, now St Michael's Hospital, where a building reminiscent of nearby Blickling was erected.

Strict regulations were enforced to discourage people from applying for help. The aim of the Poor Law Amendment Act was to cut the cost of relief and by 1840 expenditure was down by 40 per cent. The farmer-guardians in rural unions were reluctant to send married men of good character to the workhouse because of the inconvenience which they faced as employers in retrieving them when the weather improved and ploughing and sowing needed to be put in hand. This meant that doles were often reintroduced, disguised under the title 'in aid of sickness', where help at home was still permissible. In fact, by 1841 only six per cent of those in the workhouse were able-bodied. About half the inhabitants of workhouses in Norfolk were children and they may well have received a better education inside than out. Efforts to remove children from the very restrictive institutional atmosphere began in the late 19th century when they were often sent to the local school, unfortunately usually in the distinctive workhouse uniform. A more forward-looking idea was to establish foster homes; by 1900, 200 children in Norfolk were fostered.

In spite of the rule forbidding the giving of doles and pensions to people in their homes, the elderly were often helped until they could no longer look after themselves. By the 1860s there were cottages attached to the workhouse at Gressenhall for elderly

55. Children at Gressenhall school in 1912. The children from Mitford and Launditch Union Workhouse attended the school and the workhouse boys can be distinguished by their closely cropped hair and uniform jackets.

couples. All the same, many had little to look forward to except ending their days in the workhouse, and even the little comforts that crept in, such as tea and tobacco, could not remove the stigma of thriftlessness that went with the workhouse.

A more positive role of the Poor Law Union was in the provision of medical help. Qualified medical officers were appointed by the Union, but there was always a delay before they were allowed to visit a sick person. A certificate had first to be obtained from the relieving officer and these notes were issued on the grounds of the income of the sick person rather than the seriousness of the illness. The Poor Law medical officers were more successful in their vaccination work against smallpox.

By 1850, as a result of a stabilising rural population, increasing farming prosperity and, perhaps, the introduction of the new Poor Law, the farm worker's lot began to improve. Agricultural labourers had been mainly a casual workforce, fully employed only at harvest time. This had been a situation that suited the farmers but, with the drift of workers to the towns and colonies, a smaller and more regularly employed workforce came into being. The legal control of gangs and the introduction of compulsory education in the 1870s reduced the availability of women and children. Fewer women worked on the land as the demand for domestic servants by the expanding middle-class grew. By 1900, the labourer was in a far stronger position as the huge casual reserves disappeared and there were even seasonal labour shortages.

56. Friendly Societies were an important social focus for the village and often the forerunners of local trades union branches. This photograph, taken in the 1880s, shows the 'Foresters' in Banham at the start of a procession.

The period after 1850 saw the growth of trade unions in many industries, but the unions were much slower to develop in agriculture. The crisis came as wheat prices began to fall from 1870 and so farmers began to reduce wages. This coincided with riots in Swaffham and Fakenham when enclosure acts were finally passed to end the rights of commoners on the town heaths. The leader of the fight to keep the commons at Swaffham was Mr. Flaxman and from this grew the Association for the Defence of the

Rights of the Poor, which in turn became Flaxman's Eastern Counties' Union. Stirrings such as these were seen all over England and finally, in April 1872, Joseph Arch's National Agricultural Labourers' Union was founded. By the summer of 1872, there were branches across Norfolk. Membership grew through the winter, but local unions also emerged which tried to set up rival local branches. Flaxman's union had collapsed by the end of 1873, but the Lincolnshire Labourers' League was recruiting members alongside Arch's union. Many independent unions were also formed as the movement swept the county like a massive religious revival.

Inevitably, unions were disliked by farmers. One wrote, 'I believe that on every farm there is one man appointed to look and see that there is not too much work done. Whenever I find that man he always goes.' However, the farmers need not have worried; all the efforts to form unions had failed by 1878. Strikes were very difficult to organise when the workforce was so scattered. Many labourers lived in tied cottages and so feared the loss of their homes, and by 1896 this first phase of unionism was over. It was not until 1906 that further attempts were made to form unions in the countryside. This second phase was very different from the first. It lacked the 'religious' conviction, as the chapel was no longer seen as automatically representing the interests of the poor; instead it had become respectable. The founding of the new Eastern Counties' Agricultural Labourers' and Small Holders' Union was supported by the Liberal grandees within the county and to begin with the union emphasised the promotion of schemes for small holdings and improving rural conditions, especially housing, rather than the question of wages. Not until after 1910 did this change, when the union became more militant and concerned with wages. The influence of the new Independent Labour Party was increasing, but there was little real attempt to contest the political control of liberalism in rural areas until after 1914.

In spite of the failure of unions, the farm labourer's lot continued to improve in the 1870s. Even with a cut in wages, the fall in wheat prices was such that the cost of living was declining and little luxuries began to find their way into the cottages. Factory-made china ornaments as well as tobacco and tea were reaching the remotest villages as the influence of the towns became more and more obvious in the countryside.

Chapter Six
Cottages, Schools and Chapels

57. An early 19th-century survey of the Houghton estate revealed that many of the cottages were in bad repair with sagging thatched roofs. The lower drawing shows that the right-hand wall had to be shored up. There was rarely a second floor. More often, the upper rooms were in the roof with a dormer window.

The general filth and dilapidation is probably the first thing that would strike a 20th-century visitor to an early 19th-century village. Its straggling thatched and clay-lump cottages resembled the mud huts of a third-world settlement rather than a modern western European one. The cottages themselves were often in bad repair with contemporary descriptions and pictures revealing leaking roofs, sagging walls and broken windows. In some villages, this degree of dilapidation remained until the 1880s. The Rev. Jessopp described the conditions in which one of his parishioners in Scarning lived. 'A while ago, I paid a call on Mrs. Grimbly. I found her cowering over a wretched fire that could hardly keep alight and she was reading a tract in the great chimney corner and she was holding over her head a large umbrella to protect her from the rain; the miserable hovel was full of smoke, the fire was spluttering with the big rain drops that came down the vast chimney steadily and heavily.'

Behind the cottages, pigs and hens were kept and the dung heap was never far from the back door. The lack of gutters and drains meant that great pools of water would collect in wet weather. Privy arrangements were very inadequate; pumps and wells were often shared by a large number of cottages. Cholera and typhus were as much a danger in the countryside as in the towns. The upkeep of roads was a much neglected parish responsibility; they were rough and pot-holed as well as being a convenient place to dump rubbish.

In Norfolk, the village was often some distance from the church, but even where the church was central to the houses, it was often as derelict as the cottages around it. Early 19th-century engravings of Norfolk churches show many covered with ivy and partly roofless and ruinous. It was not until after 1850 that the general enthusiasm for church restoration which accompanied the Gothic revival reached the countryside.

Other buildings which were to become more typical of the village as the century wore on were the school and the chapel, but only a few of these pre-date the Victorian era. Their buildings brought some solid, often monumental architecture to the existing ramshackle village street. Very rarely was the great house of the squire visible from the village. Usually it was away within its park, protected by a wall and a belt of trees.

Conditions improved only slowly during the 19th century. Groups of model cottages were built at Holkham between 1817 and 1821 which had three bedrooms upstairs, and a pantry, kitchen and living room downstairs, but these were exceptional and the state of the cottages depended very much on the local landowner. He was under very little pressure from the tenant farmer to provide cottages for labourers; the farmer was usually the rate payer and he would want to prevent more potential claimants, or 'paupers' as they were called, from settling within his parish. The tenant would therefore ask for good farm buildings but not good cottages. Not all land agents agreed with this callous policy. Nathaniel Kent, while working at Holkham in the 1790s, wrote, 'I think it is as necessary to provide plain and comfortable cottages for the poor as to provide plain, comfortable and convenient buildings for cattle.' His motives were professional rather than humanitarian; a well-housed workforce was less likely to riot.

Two mid-19th-century descriptions survive to tell us something of cottage conditions within the county at this time. Firstly there is a survey of cottages on the Holkham estate made by the agent in 1851 and secondly there is a series of articles in the *Norfolk News* entitled 'The Cottage Homes of England', published in 1863-4, which described the cottages on several Norfolk estates.

The Holkham survey reveals how, even on a particularly well-managed estate, conditions away from the entrance to the park itself were very bad indeed. Descriptions such as 'a most wretched cottage', 'rain comes in', and 'unfit to live in', are typical while more rarely the comment, 'small, but comfortable cottage', is found. It was not only the old cottages that were badly laid out and in poor condition; of six new ones, four were defective and of a row at Dunton near Fakenham the land agent wrote, 'Though they are not by any means what labourers' cottages should be, there are numbers on the estate in a worse condition'. Most of the cottages were small. Only two had more than three bedrooms; 138 had two, 98 had one and eight had only one room.

Almost exactly the same sort of conditions were revealed in the *Norfolk News* articles. Nearly all speak of dilapidation. Conditions were worst in the areas where clay-lump building was prevalent. In one village the reporter saw 'little else but thatched roofs, old rotten and shapeless, full of holes and overgrown with weeds, windows sometimes patched with rags and sometimes plastered with clay; the walls are nearly all of clay, full of cracks and crannies.' It is not surprising that epidemics often broke out in these conditions. At Corpusty 'fever was prevalent', while in many villages such as Tittleshall there were outbreaks of cholera in the 1840s and '50s.

In some areas, cottages received more favourable comment. Those owned by Mr. Brampton Gurdon on his 4-5,000-acre estate around Cranworth were said to be well thatched and whitewashed with good gardens and at least two bedrooms. Lord Walsingham's cottages were also said to be in reasonable repair, but he very much resented the comments he received and wrote to the *Norfolk News* to criticise the secretive way in which the reporters had gone about their work. He suggested that they would have gained a fairer impression if they had called at the estate office and spoken to the agent.

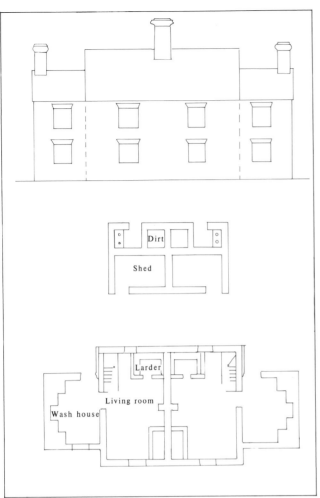

58. Plan, redrawn from an old book of drawings, of a cottage erected on the Holkham estate in the 1850s.

Dirt

Shed

Larder

Living room

Wash house

59. Early 19th-century estate cottages at Lexham. The central section is probably older than the end wings.

'They would have learnt that during the last few years many new and excellent cottages have been built in addition to those which before existed, and others have been enlarged.'

Very few farm labourers owned their own cottages, even in villages not dominated by a single landlord, and the few that did enjoyed a rare security not shared by many of their contemporaries. Those who were least secure lived in cottages supplied by the farmer for whom they worked but, when cottage rentals for Norfolk estates are studied, it is clear that many cottages stayed in the same hands for more than a generation, suggesting that a certain security of tenure existed in practice if not in theory. Many cottages were owned by small-scale landlords who were not the employers of their tenants; these were the ones that were usually in worst repair. The proprietors were people with a few hundred pounds to invest, but were often unable to afford improvements from the very small income that cottage property provided.

Both the *Norfolk News* and the Holkham estate report drew attention to a further problem of cottage accommodation; that of overcrowding. Mr. Clarke, the Norwich sanitary inspector, pointed out in 1863 that there was not only a need to build cottages, but to build enough good cottages. Although population was increasing by the end of the 18th century, cottage accommodation was not. In a cottage in Corpusty, there were 'two small, wretchedly ventilated and almost dark bedrooms with slanting roofs coming down almost to the floor. This miserable hovel was occupied by J. R., his wife, five children and their grandfather beside the illegitimate child of one of the daughters.' In many cases there was also a lodger, often living in an already overcrowded house. Mr. Clarke pointed out that 'these lodgers must be working on the land and therefore required by the estate, but no houses are provided for them. These lodgers are not a class that should exist permanently in a country village.' One single-bedroomed cottage in Flitcham was occupied by two families and three lodgers. Lord Walsingham claimed that lodgers were not allowed in his cottages and wrote to the *Norfolk News*: 'The case of the lodger is contrary to all regulations and if known would have been put an end to.'

Even with this degree of overcrowding, not enough labour to work the farms could be found within estate-controlled parishes. All except the very young and very old could hope for employment at least at harvest time. Child and female labour was particularly in demand because it was cheaper. The possible loss of child labour was the main reason why farmers were against compulsory education. Lord Leicester's attitude towards juvenile labour seems to have been typical of that of employers. He thought that boys of ten should work, although in 1867 he claimed that he would support a law prohibiting the employment of children under that age. If there was such a law, he 'need not succumb to the solicitations of parents'. Neither did he approve of the employment of women under 20, 'but female labour cannot altogether be dispensed with in this neighbourhood'. In Tittleshall in 1851, 14 boys between the ages of five and 14 were regularly employed. Only four girls under 14 were permanently employed and 22 women were described as farm labourers. In the days before pensions men worked for as long as they could find an employer and in Tittleshall there were four labourers in their 70s and one 82-year-old.

With all the family employed, Lord Leicester reckoned that two cottages were needed for every 100 acres, but he admitted that on the Holkham estate the provision was far lower than this.

To make up for the lack of labour living locally, farmers employed gangs recruited in the surrounding villages not so tightly controlled by a single landlord, where small speculators had put up cottages. There was much criticism and many scandals associated with this practice, and in 1843 a Royal Commission looked into the working of the gang system and the injustices that resulted. The Victorian middle-class conscience was moved by the idea of gangs of men, women and children walking long distances to work and then working together in the fields, often under an unscrupulous gang master, for very low wages. Farmers on the other hand argued that the seasonal nature of much of the work made the employment of gangs necessary. Some of the worst abuses of the system were stopped after 1845 when gangs had to be licensed.

60.   These cottages at Egmere are part of a group built between 1878 and 1880. Egmere had been particularly short of cottages, relying on labourers walking from Walsingham, but changes in the rating system stimulated a building programme. They are of interest because they are built of shuttered concrete, an experiment in new materials which was neither long-lived nor very successful.

The main reason for the lack of cottage building was the desire to prevent any population rise which might result in an increase in the burden of the Poor Rate. Even though workhouse and poor relief were organised by the Union, each parish had to pay individually for those from the parish who called on its help. After 1865 this changed and a rate was set for the entire Union regardless of how many paupers came from each parish. This meant there was now no advantage in individual parishes keeping down numbers. As a result, cottage building increased. This period of building activity coincided with a steadying of the population, and by the end of the century conditions were improving and overcrowding was coming to an end. Yet, in spite of the rash of substantial terraced and semi-detached brick cottages with their date stones and family crests which were springing up in estate villages from the mid-1860s, there was still much squalor. As late as 1887, Augustus Jessopp wrote, 'There may be some excuse for the hideous crowding of human beings in towns; there is no excuse for it in the country where land is sold by the acre, not the square inch.' It was the lack of clean water and sanitation that was particularly obvious. Jessopp was struck by the incongruity of the fact that by this date towns were better supplied with water, and indeed milk, than was the countryside.

Even on the largest estates there were still horrors in the 1890s. A great deal of repair and building was needed on the Gunton estate and one cottage, described in 1894 as 'beyond repair', had seven occupants and only one bedroom which was on the ground floor. Jessopp blamed the fact that people were leaving the countryside partly on the poor housing. Also, of course, wages in the towns were higher and there was a greater chance of improving one's position in a job with the prospect of promotion. The police force was a career which appealed to many a country lad. It was the spread of education in the countryside which increased the awareness amongst young people of the existence of better prospects elsewhere and made them keen to leave their home villages.

The development of rural education, which ensured that by 1900 most country people could read and write, was a great achievement of the 19th century. There were many motives behind this drive for literacy and numeracy, one of which was the creation of a law-abiding, Bible-reading society. In 1834 the Bishop of London said in evidence to a Select Committee on education, 'In riots in agricultural districts, the most violent men are always the most illiterate'.

By the early 19th century it was obvious that the few endowed schools along with the various dame schools could not provide for all educational needs and the church was seen as the most suitable body to fill the gap. As a result, by 1820, two societies for education had been founded; the National Society for Promoting the Education of the Poor was supported by the Church of England, and the British and Foreign Bible Society by the nonconformists. Thus began a rivalry over the control of education between the various religious denominations which was to bedevil progress towards state involvement over the next 50 years.

The first Select Committtee on Education reported in 1816 and listed 100 endowed schools as well as 589 others in Norfolk. Many of these were very small and impermanent dame schools. However, it did mean that well over half the parishes in Norfolk had some sort of school, although 76 only had a Sunday school. Over the next 20 years the number of schools grew steadily as a

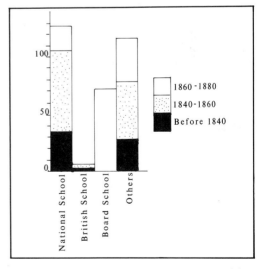

61. Graph showing the growth in the provision of elementary education in Norfolk. British schools were rarely found outside towns, which explains why there were so few in Norfolk.

result of support from both the religious societies and the local landowners. Between 1840 and 1873 grants were available from the Privy Council to help finance the building or enlarging of schools and, as a result, 130 new schools were built with the help of grants while about 50 were erected entirely at the expense of the landlord or rector.

Once the schools had been built, the main problem was to encourage children to stay long enough for their education to make any progress. If fieldwork was available it is hardly surprising that parents with low incomes wanted their children to be at work. Only very slowly did the old idea of the child as a small worker, who must begin to contribute to the family income as soon as possible, begin to disappear. In the middle of the century three children over eight years old could double the weekly family income. The result was that, over much of the agricultural area of eastern England, only about one-eighth of the children who attended school spent more than 200 days a year there. The rector of Banham wrote in 1852, 'The children leave school very early for field work. Almost all come to school for a time. Few stay long enough to acquire anything worthy of the name of education.'

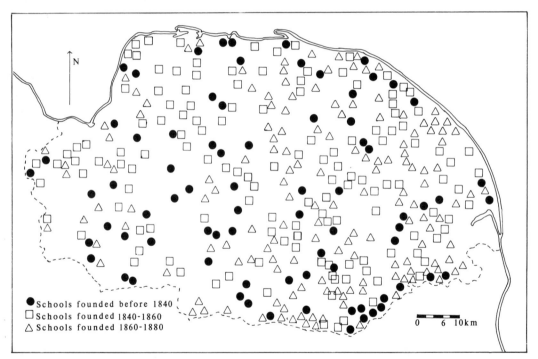

62. This map of Norfolk shows the date at which different schools were founded and how limited was the provision of schools before 1840. They seem to have been fairly evenly distributed across the county, with a concentration along the River Waveney in the south.

Finally, in 1870 the Forster Education Act provided for the setting up of School Boards to establish schools where the already existing voluntary schools did not provide enough places for all the children in an area. From 1876 parents were compelled to see that their children received an education, but school attendance was very difficult to enforce, particularly when magistrate farmers wanted child labour and parents wanted money. Feelings towards the setting up of School Boards were mixed. Most of the National and Voluntary schools established after 1870 were in villages where the existence of a School Board was resented. Some landowners, however, had no objection to sharing the expense of a school with other rate payers, especially when most of the members of the Board might well be his tenants. The Earl of Leicester and his estate office at Holkham gave much assistance in the setting up of the Castle Acre and Wells School Boards, and Samuel Shallabear, the agent, became chairman of the Wells Board.

The largest landowners all built at least one school on their estates, usually in the villages nearest their Hall. For instance, the Marquis of Cholmondeley built one for the Birchams in 1847. He continued to support it and partly clothed the children. The Marquis of Lothian supported Blickling school and Lord Suffield built the elegant little school at Antingham in 1826. The smaller landowners, too, all built and supported their own village school and all these establishments were seen as something of a status symbol by their benefactors. Coats of arms were often put over the door and elaborate ecclesiastical designs were frequently chosen. These Gothic, Tudor and classical buildings with their lofty rooms were not very practical as schools, but that was not necessarily important to their benefactors.

Formal school education seems to have been unattractive to many of those subjected to it. George Baldry recalled in *The Rabbit Skin Cap* that he remembered little from his one year of schooling beyond the religious teaching. Without any parental support, teachers often felt their task to be very difficult and excuses for the non-attendance of children were many. Despite the restrictive curriculum, some young scholars did gain a taste for reading and, in many villages, reading rooms and literary institutions were widely supported and evening lectures enthusiastically attended. George Edwards, a child in the 1840s and later an agricultural trade union leader, did not go to school but was taught to read by his wife. Once he had learned, his appetite for reading was great, and this must have been true of many other intelligent young men of his generation. Servants in some of the great houses were encouraged to read by the provision of a servants' library. At Blickling this contained religious works as well as books of legends and biographies of exemplary people.

If the main aims of Victorian mass education were to lay in children's minds the foundations of obedience to their governors and to make them contented in their stations, then it failed. Instead many former pupils later acted as lay preachers for the dissenting, particularly Primitive Methodist, chapels; they set up trade unions and eventually some became involved in politics.

At the beginning of the 19th century the one building that still dominated the village was the church. The fact that many were half ruined and in need of repair reflected the century of religious apathy that had gone before. Many of the problems of the Anglican church were inherited from the Middle Ages, and it was not until the 1830s that the ancient institutions that had governed the church were modernised. The state of the local church depended largely on the amount of interest shown by the bishop. In 18th-century Norfolk there was no effective leadership given by the prelates, many of whom only held the office for a few years while others were non-resident. The Bishop of Norwich from 1806-37 was Bishop Bathurst, a cultured Whig gentleman and the only

63. Welborne National School, built in 1847 beside the church and attended by about 40 children.

64. Interior of Swaffham elementary school, 1911. This photograph shows the arrangement of desks and the children's work around the wall.

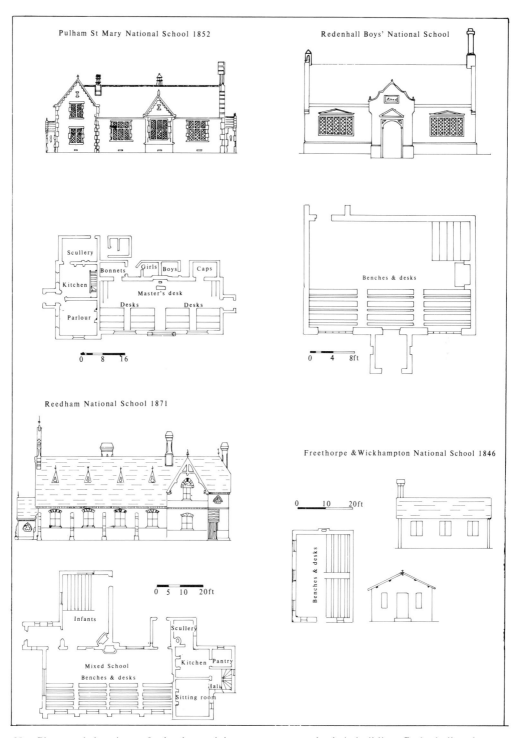

Pulham St Mary National School 1852

Redenhall Boys' National School

Scullery

Kitchen

Bonnets

Girls Boys

Caps

Master's desk

Desks

Desks

Parlour

0   8   16

Benches & desks

0   4   8ft

Reedham National School 1871

Freethorpe & Wickhampton National School 1846

0   10   20ft

Infants

Scullery

0   5   10   20ft

Kitchen   Pantry

Mixed School

Benches & desks

Hall

Sitting room

Benches & desks

65.   Plans and drawings of schools receiving a grant towards their building. Redenhall and
Freethorpe-with-Wickhampton are both single-roomed buildings while Pulham St Mary and
Reedham incorporate a teacher's house. In Reedham the infants were taught separately, while at
Pulham and Redenhall the infants would have occupied the desks in front and beside the master.
The desks and benches of the main school were always placed along the length of the building,
allowing a large space in front of the master for recitation and the teaching of small groups of
pupils.

bishop to support the 1828 Bill giving Roman Catholics political and civil rights. He died at the age of 93 and for the last years of his life had been incapable of discharging his duties, spending much of his time taking the spa waters at Bath. His death left the way open for reform and the new bishop, Edward Stanley, was responsible for many changes within the diocese.

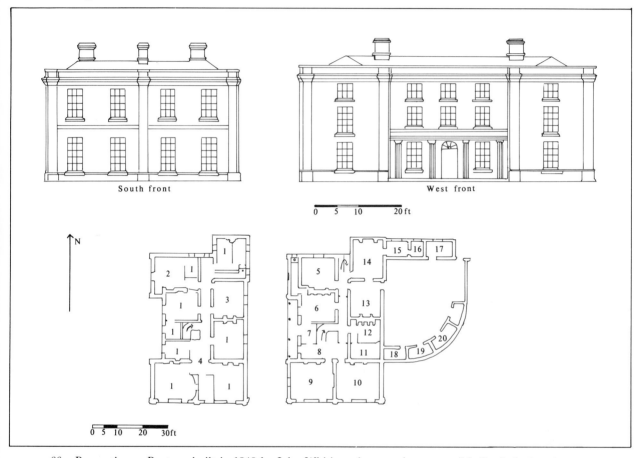

66. Baconsthorpe Rectory, built in 1840 by John Whiting who was also responsible for designing those at Letheringset and Poringland.

Key	1. Bedroom	8. Hall	15. Cooks' pantry
	2. School room	9. Dining room	16. Larder
	3. Nursery	10. Drawing room	17. Coal
	4. Landing	11. Store	18. Dairy
	5. Servants' hall	12. Pantry	19. Knives
	6. Study	13. Scullery	20. Firing
	7. Vestibule	14. Kitchen	

Firstly there was the problem of non-residence. When Edward Stanley arrived, as many as 500 clergy lived outside their parishes. The main reason for this was the lack of suitable rectories. When William Andrew became vicar of Ketteringham in 1835, there was no parsonage. The previous vicar had been more interested in politics and

67. On a less grand, but still very substantial, scale is the mid-century rectory at Mileham.

68. This interior view of Sparham rectory early this century shows the clutter of furniture and the assortment of prints and pictures so much prized by a typical middle-class family.

69. Booton church, drawn by Ladbrooke in the early 19th century and described by the Rev. Whitwell Elwin as a 'crumbling medieval building'.

70. Booton church as it was rebuilt by the Rev. Whitwell Elwin between 1876 and 1900. He designed and paid for the church himself and wrote in 1898, 'I have had but one end in view, which was to give the church the aspect of a house devoted to prayer'. Although he moved in the most eminent artistic and literary circles, he had no architectural training himself and simply copied features from churches he liked. His friend Edwin Lutyens described the building as 'very naughty but built in the right spirit'.

hunting and had held two other livings. He had rarely visited Ketteringham and eventually William Andrew had to buy himself a house in nearby Hethersett. Edward Stanley very quickly began to rectify the situation and, by 1842, 68 new rectories had been built. These varied considerably in size and style from classical to rustic and ornate gothic. By 1877, the total number of non-resident clergy had been reduced to 101. As the clergy became resident, they began to play a more important role in parish life. Several were responsible for building schools and they were nearly always school governors. Jessopp remembered that as a curate in the 1860s he had been a doctor, as there was not one for several miles. He also had to read details of legal documents, such as the terms of leases, to the illiterate. 'My experience ranged from writing a letter to making a will and from setting a bone to stopping a suicide.'

The clergy also became concerned over the appearance of their churches and the form of services that went on inside them. By the middle of the 19th century an enthusiasm for 'gothic' and a pride in church fabric resulted in a great restoration movement. Landlord and vicar often worked side by side in this, with many landlords providing most of the money. Jessopp thought that between 1840 and 1879 about 860 churches in Norfolk were built or rebuilt at a cost of about £900,000. (This figure included the new suburban churches around Norwich and elsewhere as well as the country parishes, but it is still a very impressive sum.)

Resident clergy ensured that services were held regularly and became less formal in character. Hymn singing became an accepted part of the church service and organs and surpliced choirs were introduced. The changes were often initially regarded with suspicion, but were usually accepted and eventually acknowledged to be an improvement.

Diaries such as those kept by the Rev. Andrew of Ketteringham and the Rev. Armstrong of East Dereham show the new style of conscientious clergy at work. William Andrew was a dedicated evangelist who was very critical of the equally strong-minded squire, Sir John Boileau. He felt that Sir John did not show the reverence he should for the Sabbath and disapproved of his support for the theatre and his acceptance of a stewardship at the Norwich races. Sir John on the other hand thought that one sermon on a Sunday was enough, while Andrew insisted on preaching two. In spite of the troubles, Rev. Andrew succeeded in creating a regular church life in Ketteringham which had previously been served by non-resident clergy with no interest in the parish.

Benjamin Armstrong went to East Dereham in 1851 and wrote of the neighbouring clergy, 'Indifferentism is the prevailing feeling among them, and the farm, the Petty Sessions or the Union Board are their occupation. They live like educated and well disposed gentlemen and seem to have no taste for the work of the ministry.' He, however, was very concerned with parish matters and, by his death, church services were well organised and frequent; the church was seen to be closely involved in local affairs.

The late 18th-century Anglican church had been shocked out of its lethargy by the rise of nonconformity, particularly the new Methodist movement. John Wesley first came to Norwich in 1754, and by 1790 he had visited the county at least 40 times. Gradually, circuits linking the various groups set up in the towns and villages were established; by 1800 there were six circuits in Norfolk based on Norwich (1765), Lynn (1776), Yarmouth (1786), Diss (1790), Walsingham (1791) and Thetford (1797). Most groups started by meeting in houses and only after they had been established some time did they build chapels.

71. Guestwick Independent chapel, exterior. This chapel was originally founded at the end of the Cromwellian Commonwealth and some of the interior beams may date from then. However, in 1833 the Rev. Drane, the minister, prepared plans for the complete restoration of the building and most of the present chapel dates from that time. It was reopened for public worship in 1840.

72. This interior photograph of Guestwick chapel shows the typical early layout of an Independent meeting house, with its gallery and box pews coming right up to the minister's pulpit, giving a great feeling of intimacy and communion between the minister and worshippers.

The story of Themelthorpe chapel is typical of many: the founder of the group was Rebecca Yarham who moved with her husband and daughters to a small farm in the parish in 1811. When she first arrived, 'such was the spiritual destitution of the place that she felt as lone as a sparrow on a roof top'. Some of the villagers attended the one service 'conducted at the parish church on the Sabbath, but most of the sacred day was spent by the young men on the common in all kinds of games, while their seniors gossiped and read newspapers in the public house'. Meanwhile, Rebecca and her children walked three miles to the nearest chapel every Sunday. After 1821 she opened her house for meetings and blind Billy Rudd, a local preacher from Reepham, came every week. For some years after Rebecca's death the group had no leader, but it was later restarted and by 1889 had outgrown the farmhouse kitchen and a fund was opened for the building of a chapel.

73. The interior of Blo Norton Methodist chapel, *c.*1900.

After John Wesley's death the Methodists lacked a good leader and became embroiled in internal conflicts which resulted in various breakaway sects. Expansion between 1800 and 1850 was slower than it had been in earlier years. The most important of these breakaway groups was the Primitive Methodists founded by Hugh Bourne in Tunstall

74. Two late 19th-century chapel buildings at Fincham. The right-hand one was the Sunday school.

(Staffordshire) in 1811. Their very free form of worship in the open air was frowned upon by central authority, and those who wanted to continue using these evangelical methods broke away from the main body of the Wesleyan movement. The Primitive Methodists reached Norfolk in the 1820s and by 1851 had nearly as many chapels as all the other Wesleyan groups put together. It was the simplicity and directness of their preaching that impressed observers. Many preachers such as the trade unionist, George Edwards, could not read or write when they started their work. He had to learn the hymns and bible readings by heart before taking the service, and it was this sort of appeal from one of their own that attracted the villagers.

All nonconformist groups continued to grow, some more slowly than others, so that by mid-century half the church-going population of England and Wales attended nonconformist chapels. This fact was brought to light by a unique survey of church attendance undertaken on Sunday 30 March 1851 as part of the 10-yearly census. The village-by-village statistics show how far the dissenters had penetrated into the countryside. Dissenting chapels were found in small, large, estate and non-estate settlements alike. Throughout the county nearly two-thirds of the population attended at least one service that Sunday. It is impossible to tell from the census returns what sort of people belonged to different sects. Sometimes the occupation of the steward who signed the form is given. Many were farmers, some were labourers, while one could not sign his name and so made his mark instead. The general picture is of a wide variety

of chapels flourishing alongside the established church, both attracting an attendance
above the national average. Very often a traditional allegiance to the parish church
meant that many dissenters worshipped there as well. In 1850, the vicar of Eccles wrote
of the dissenters in his parish, 'there are not many who do not occasionally visit the
church'.

The pulpit of the nonconformist, particularly Primitive, chapels has often been seen
as providing a training in public speaking. At least 30 per cent of the local trade union
leaders were also influential Methodists. (One of their favourite texts was Deuteronomy
25,verse 4: 'The working ox cannot be muzzled'.) As well as providing leadership, the
chapels also lent their buildings for trade union meetings. The close connection between
the chapels and the unions was also a factor in preventing violence in the early
confrontations between farmer and labourer.

During the last 20 years of the 19th century, the nonconformists were able to keep
up their numbers despite a fall in rural population. The rebuilding of village chapels
at this time, often mimicking the gothic style of the parish church, is evident from their

75. A Primitive Methodist mission van in Beetley, *c*.1900.

date stones and points to the increasing wealth and respectability of the movement which was becoming more and more embarrassed by its radical past. In some areas it has been shown that much of the early enthusiasm for the dissenters had evaporated by the 1880s, leaving the way open for the Salvation Army, but this was not true in Norfolk where the rural population remained loyal to its chapel, most usually a Primitive Methodist one.

By the end of the century conditions in the villages had improved considerably. Most farm cottages were by now two-storeyed and fairly sound. Overcrowding was greatly reduced although the provision of water and sanitation was still far behind that in towns. Improved communications, particularly the arrival of the railway, meant that the villager could visit a town more frequently and choose from a wider range of food and other goods. He was better clothed and could read and write, and, now that he could also vote, he took a far greater interest in national affairs.

The appearance of the village had also changed. The church was restored and the chapel and school were newly built. Neat, if rather dull, rows of semi-detached or terraced cottages had replaced the ramshackle slums and the landlord could indeed feel that he had fulfilled the paternalistic role, which in many villages he had set for himself.

Pushed along by national trends, the community was altering, too. It was no longer a self-contained unit and the variety of employment it offered had declined. Many crafts disappeared and from 1850 the population of most villages was shrinking. The end of the Settlement Laws allowed people to travel in search of better work and many moved to the towns. However, it was not until the arrival of the internal combustion engine that the greatest changes came to village life.

Chapter Seven
Market Towns

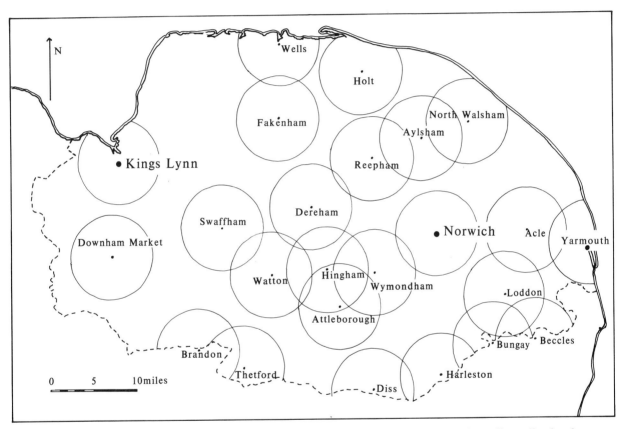

76. Map to show the distribution of market towns across Norfolk in 1850. A circle of five-miles radius has been drawn around each town, emphasising the concentration of river ports along the Waveney in the south and the relative paucity of towns in the less fertile north-west and south-west Breckland region.

The Norfolk countryside is remarkable for the number of towns with thriving weekly markets that survived into this century. Originating in the Middle Ages, as their medieval churches and market places show, they were the vehicles by which influences from the outside world reached the countryside. Roads were poor and about four miles was as far as traders could walk with their goods and livestock to market and so, over much of Norfolk, market towns are about eight to ten miles apart. Because water was an important method of transport until the introduction of the railways, markets are

81

found clustered along the river valleys and the north coast. It is clear that even as early as the Middle Ages, Norwich and Kings Lynn were important regional centres as no towns are found in their immediate vicinity, while towns are more densely packed in the fertile east and more sparse in the west of the county.

The early prosperity of these towns had been based on sheep. Generations of cloth, yarn and wool merchants had brought their business to them and this traditional trade still continued in some towns in the 19th century. There were a few looms working in Aylsham for Norwich firms in the 1850s while in Dereham, although there was no weaving, there was spinning and wool combing and the town was still noted for its wool market. Wymondham was a centre for weaving bombasines and crêpe, with over 600 looms at the beginning of the century; by 1850, there were only 120, mostly working for Norwich firms. The Waveney valley hemp and linen industry was centred on Diss. Although the industry was in decline by the 1830s, the Royal Commission investigating handloom weaving found there was more work in Diss than in other areas. 'From evidence obtained in Diss, there is good reason to believe that the weavers of Haverhill, where 100 looms are idle, might do much work if they exerted themselves.' Weaving at the once famous centre of Worstead had long since ended: 'Formerly a town of consequence and celebrated as the first seat of manufacture of worsted stuffs, it is now reduced to the rank of an agricultural village.'

77. Swaffham market place with the 18th-century cross in the foreground and the Corn Hall, built in 1858, beyond. The ground floor contained a billiard room, reading room and library and the large upper room was occasionally let. The Assembly Rooms were in the white-washed building to the left of the picture.

Horse hair weaving was a speciality of Wymondham where it continued into the 20th century, and Rattle Row in the town was so called because of the sound of the noisy looms from the upper rooms of the terraced houses. A letter of 1846 describes the 'ghastly rows of tumble-down dwellings' occupied chiefly by handloom weavers 'where shuttles may be heard with a monotonous click-clack in their upper rooms'.

Several Norfolk towns had also been renowned for the butter trade. At Watton, for instance, 'immense quantities [of butter] were purchased weekly and sent by factors to London'. The butter market in Swaffham was erected in 1783 to provide cool shelter for dairy products. At Downham Market, the large butter market was 'now obsolete [1850], the growing of corn and wool and the feeding of cattle now being more important in these parts'.

In spite of the decline in the wool and dairy trades the market towns continued to flourish throughout the 19th century. The weekly markets, held in the spacious market places, sold mainly provisions while some such as Fakenham, Dereham, Reepham, Diss and Docking held auctions of smaller livestock such as pigs and poultry. In the public houses around the market places, often sporting elegant Georgian frontages, although much older behind, the corn merchants and maltsters would be available to see samples of the crop the farmers might bring in, going from one to another, seeking the highest price.

From the 1840s companies were set up to build corn halls and, over the next ten years, eight were built in the major market centres. These imposing buildings varied from classical to Byzantine in style, always having a sheaf of wheat on their facades. The merchants met their clients there rather than in the inns and the buildings could also be used as assembly rooms and for public meetings. In 1879 the vicar of Dereham was scandalised to hear that an entertainment was to be given by 'Madame Card' in the corn hall on Good Friday and managed to get the event moved to Easter Monday instead, not entirely to the satisfaction of the 'mesmeric enchantress' who thought that, as the Prince of Wales was opening a hospital in Hunstanton on that day, the holiday makers might be tempted there instead.

The decline in the importance of wheat after 1880 meant that the useful life of corn halls was rather short, but most of them still stand, adding dignity, if sometimes of a rather decaying nature, to their market places. The Swaffham Corn Hall is now the Job Centre, while the one in Dereham is a cinema.

More important for the sale of cattle, sheep and horses were the 'fairs'. Some towns such as Watton had as many as five annually, three for cattle, one for sheep and one for all types of stock. Hingham was described as having three 'large stock fairs' and Thetford was the only place where a wool fair, held after shearing time in late June-early July, still survived. Diss had the only lamb fair, in November. Other than these, fairs were described as for 'stock' although occasionally there was 'peddlary' as well. Pleasure fairs were held at Attleborough and Wells mid-century and seven hiring fairs still took place at or around Michaelmas for the hiring of farm labourers and servants. At Aylsham, this was followed by a fair for 'peddlary and clothing, when servants can renew their apparel'.

By the 19th century shops were growing up around the market places. In North Walsham, for instance, by 1850 butter and poultry were sold direct to the shops and inns rather than through the market, and most market towns could boast a wide variety of shops. Thetford was described as having 'many handsome shops'. Dereham had 'several long streets lined with neat modern shops'. A great variety of goods would have been sold in all the towns. Gradually, through the 19th century, many crafts were becoming town- rather than village-based. There were still boot and shoe makers and blacksmiths to be found in most villages, but clothing was mainly bought in the towns. Tailors, hat makers (both milliners and straw hat makers), dress makers and drapers became increasingly town-based.

78. An engraving of Dereham Corn Hall, erected in 1856 and large enough to seat 1,000 people.

79. Norwich Horse Fair in the early years of this century, held in the cattle market below the castle.

80.   Dereham on market day, *c*.1900.

81.   Dereham fair was a twice-yearly event, in July and September. This photograph must date from *c*.1900.

Although some country blacksmiths developed into agricultural engineers and ironsmiths, these were mainly to be found in the towns, especially after the coming of the railways which made the transport of coal and iron to the areas around the stations easier. Many of the larger towns had more than one iron foundry. Plowrights of Swaffham, Randells of North Walsham, the Farmers Foundry at Great Ryburgh, near Fakenham, and Cornish's iron works at Walsingham all made a wide variety of farm implements and household goods sold throughout the county; many a farmyard has pig troughs in use today with the names of these foundries stamped on the side. Burrells of Thetford began in 1770 as a general smithy and grew to produce the world's first heavy-duty traction engine in 1856; over 4,000 traction engines were made there before 1914. The firm also specialised in showmen's road locomotives and produced a wide variety of agricultural machinery.

Farmers coming to the weekly market not only needed to buy agricultural implements; they also needed the professional services of auctioneers, attorneys, banks and insurance offices, all of which were to be found there. Towns also had their basket makers, book sellers, brewers, brass and tin smiths, cabinet makers and chemists, while the everyday needs of both town and country would be served by numerous butchers, bakers, fishmongers, grocers and confectioners. The requirements of horses were met by harness and saddle makers as well as farriers. Most of the goods sold would have been made, or in the case of grocers, packaged, on the premises. While market day would undoubtedly have been the busiest, local trade in perishable goods would have been brisk all week. Shops were open long hours and craftsmen worked even longer in the back of their shops. Gradually, as the century wore on, more goods such as those in the ironmonger's would have been factory made, but most crafts survived into the present century.

As well as shops, most market towns supported several industries. There were iron foundries, breweries and either steam- or water-powered corn mills in all major towns. Watton brewery was set up in 1809 in buildings that still stand, while the impressive buildings of Bidwell's brewery and maltings in Thetford were demolished in the 1950s. Dereham, on the main crossing point of the north-south and east-west railway route by 1850, quickly became the largest malting centre in Norfolk. As well as this, by mid-century it had a sack factory and steam saw mill beside the line and in the 1850s the little church of St Withberga was built to serve the growing population along the Norwich road beyond the station. With the arrival of the railway in Watton in 1869, coal, corn and cattle feed businesses were set up along the track, employing as many as 80 people.

Many towns had their own specialist activities. Wymondham was known as a centre for the manufacture of turned wooden products such as spoons and spindles and also for the production of brushes, both of which occupations were concentrated in factories by 1880. There was a paper mill in Thetford in 1850, employing 60 people, and in 1879 the pulp mill producing papier maché-type household goods such as bowls, described as 'light, durable, waterproof and quiet to use', was founded. Diss also had two brush factories as well as a company making coconut matting.

Although all market towns had much in common, they varied in size and importance. The top ten all had populations over 2,000 by mid-century and Dereham, Wymondham and Thetford had over 4,000 inhabitants. It was the railway which accounted for the

82. Dereham High Street, lined with shops. The locksmith on the left has a large padlock shop sign hanging over his premises.

83. Workers beside the cupola, Farmers' Foundry, Great Ryburgh.

84. Maltings beside the railway, Dereham.

continued growth of Dereham, while Thetford's development had been based on water transport along the Thetford navigation. Eight staunches had been built on the Little Ouse to maintain depths, and tolls were charged throughout the 19th century. Fisons opened a riverside factory for the manufacture of fertilisers in 1853. The importance of the navigation declined with the development of the railway system and Thetford's population dropped between 1861 and 1871. Wymondham began to suffer from its proximity to Norwich and, after 1851, its population, too, began to decline. By 1881 the market there was 'almost extinct owing to the great facilities provided by the railway for attending Norwich market'.

Of the other towns with a population over 2,000 in 1851, only one suffered a drop in population before 1900: this was Wells. With the development of railways, the import-ance of coastal traffic declined and the trade of Wells harbour suffered accordingly. In contrast, the population of North Walsham rose sharply with the arrival of the railway, and its industries, particularly iron founding, expanded. In 1881 it was noted of North Walsham, 'extensive granaries and ware houses have recently been built ajoining the railways'.

The population of the smaller market towns remained fairly static throughout the 19th century and many of them were isolated from change by the fact that they were not on a railway line. However, even if they did not spawn the rows of brick terraced

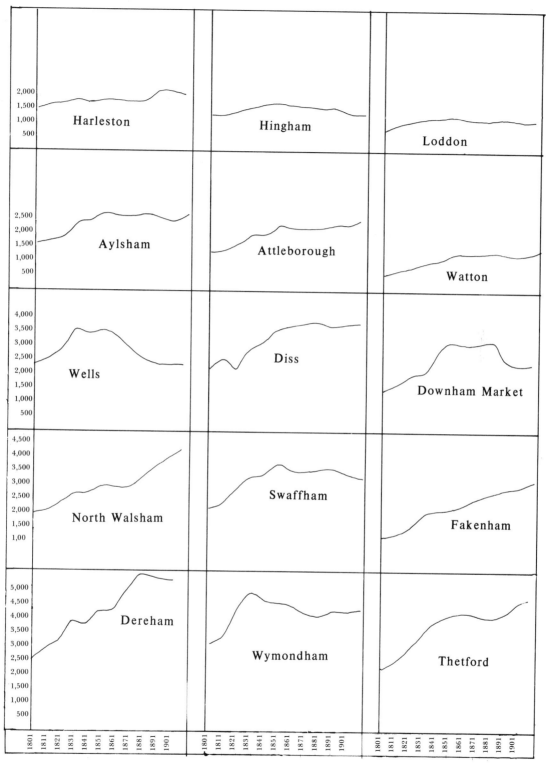

85. Population graphs for the 15 largest market towns (excluding Norwich, Yarmouth and Kings Lynn), 1801-1901.

86. High Terrace, Fakenham, built about 1890 by Mr. Uttings, a brewer from Walsall, is a very rare example of rural back-to-back housing. It provided two-storey dwellings, some with an attic room as well.

houses and 'neat villas' to be found around their expanding neighbours, they continued to serve the surrounding villages on market days and retained much of their Georgian charm into this century.

Norfolk's market towns mid-century were generally prosperous and based on a wide variety of activities serving the local community, with specialist trades serving a wider market. Conditions in many of the towns had been improving over the previous 20 years. Fakenham was described in the 1850s as having been 'greatly enlarged and improved in the last 30 years by the erection of new houses, some of them large and handsome'. North Walsham, Thetford and Dereham were also said to have smart modern houses and shops. Improvements in Dereham, which had had a reputation for squalor, were particularly impressive. One advance which had taken place in most towns between 1830 and 1850 was the setting up of gas companies. The earliest, at Diss, was set up in 1835, and by 1850 nearly all the towns were lit by gaslight.

Cholera, however, was still feared in Norfolk towns as elsewhere and in 1851

87a-d. Four interior views at High Terrace taken shortly before demolition. The stone sink, kitchen range and bedroom fire place are surely original fittings.

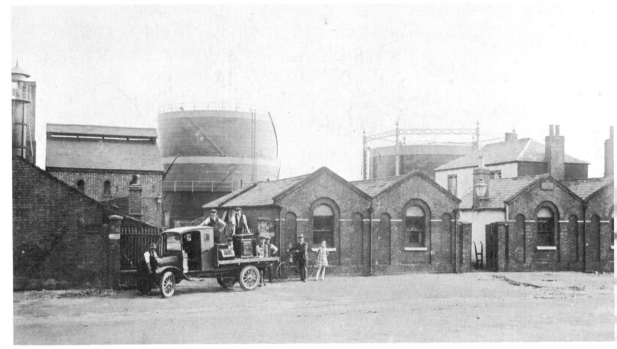

88.   Fakenham Gasworks was set up in 1846 and enlarged in 1856 when the retort house, on the left of this 1920s photograph, was probably built. The buildings still stand and are the only surviving example of a small-town gasworks. They are now preserved as a museum.

Aylsham Vestry Committee reported on the inadequacy of drains. There were numerous uncovered cess pools, open drains and dung heaps in some of the most populated parts. A medical report on conditions in Thetford in the 1860s stated, 'Scarcely any of the conditions necessary to the health and well being of an urban population are found'. There was no proper system of drainage and the smell of the tannery pervaded the town. Water supply from wells was contaminated and at the *Rose and Crown* there were 18 to 20 pigs in the yard surrounded by heaps of manure. 'A well on the Bury road is three feet from a cess pit, six feet from a privy and in close proximity to the church yard.' Not surprisingly, typhoid was prevalent, but it was not until 1877 that Thetford Water Works were set up. The Rev. Armstrong of Dereham sat on the local Board of Health and, on an inspection in 1853, 'was astonished that in this, one of the prettiest and cleanest towns in England there are such fearful nuisances at the back of some of the houses. Attempts at pig and cow-keeping in a town must always be injurious and, added to the defective surface drainage, must be pestiferous.' Work on a water works and sewage system for Dereham began in 1879 when a Rural Sanitary Authority was set up. The Byzantine-style brick water tower still stands, dwarfed by the modern concrete mushroom beside it.

THE CHOLERA.

The Medical Board at Swaffham submit the following

REMARKS AND ADVICE,

Respecting the Cholera.

No disease is more easy to cure in its First Stage, or more difficult afterwards.

Cholera may be divided into three stages. First, the *Warning*; secondly, the *Attack*; and thirdly, the *Collapse*.

1st. The warning, or looseness—This always precedes Cholera, and cannot be distinguished from any other common attack of the same kind; but if you apply for medical advice in this stage, (especially within the first four hours,) the cure is easy and almost certain. In all such attacks, therefore, though you may think them of the common sort, whenever you find your bowels loose or uneasy, complain directly—all depends upon this.

2nd. The Attack, or Cramps. These generally begin in the legs and arms, and soon become extremely painful; here cure is uncertain, but still may be effected. Lose not a moment in trying to restore warmth, and getting medical aid.

3rd. The Collapse, or Blue Stage. Here the patient rapidly sinks, and recovery, though not impossible, is but seldom to be expected.

The following Medicine is recommended to be taken immediately, upon the first symptoms of attack.

Powdered Rhubarb and prepared Chalk, each ten grains, powdered Ginger five grains; to be taken in a little warm water, or Ginger tea. Avoid drinking Spirits.

This, however, is not designed to supersede applicaton to a medical man; on the contrary, the intention of the medicine is to check the disease in the first stage, till medical advice can be had, to which immediate application should be made.

SKILL, PRINTER, SWAFFHAM.

89. Poster published by Swaffham Board óf Health, explaining precautions that could be taken against cholera in the epidemic of 1832.

90. Dereham Water Tower, built by the local Water Board in 1880, with the modern water tower behind.

The Rev. Armstrong's remarks about the cows and pigs remind us that even the largest market towns were still very much part of the countryside. Some, such as Fakenham and Swaffham, retained their commons well into the second half of the 19th century. Swaffham employed a town pinder to take the town's livestock onto the commons in the morning and the pound, where unclaimed animals were put at night, survives to this day. All towns had outlying hamlets and farms within their boundaries.

By the end of the 19th century, the town was providing social services as well as marketing facilities for its neighbourhood. Thetford, North Walsham, Hingham, Swaffham, Walsingham and Holt all had grammar schools and those with boarding facilities could take boys from wealthy families in the countryside as well as the town. There were also private 'academies' for both girls and boys and there were 12 such establishments in Dereham in the 1850s, some of them very small indeed. However, they did allow the sons and daughters of local farmers to experience life in a town and away from home. Some towns built subscription cottage hospitals which provided an alternative to the workhouse infirmaries; Watton cottage hospital was founded in 1890. In Fakenham there was a nurses' home providing private nursing for those who could afford it, with a much lower rate for the poor. All towns had libraries or reading rooms, supplied with the London papers, where subscribers could keep abreast of current affairs. Most also had a theatre and social events were held in assembly rooms, corn halls and inns. Local magistrates also sat in towns and Swaffham and Thetford were assize towns which gave them added social status.

The impact of the railways on Norfolk towns has already been mentioned. For a long time the market town had been the only link between the isolated rural communities and the outside world. By the late 18th century, the stage coach from London passed

91. Theatre Royal, Dereham, shortly before demolition.

through bringing, amongst other things, newspapers, which could be read in the local inns. It was not until the arrival of the railways that it was possible for the ordinary countryman to travel beyond his local centre. Cities such as Norwich or even London were now within his reach and although most market towns continued to prosper into the railway age, they were no longer the fashionable centres for the local gentry that they had been in earlier times.

The railways themselves provided a great deal of employment. Directly, there were the railway company's employees in the stations, goods yards, on the lines and on the trains. Indirectly, there were the carriers linking outlying villages with the railways. The numerous *Railway Taverns* with their stables beside them are a reminder of the need to look after horses between journeys. Most stations were a little way from the old town centres, and new housing and industrial areas grew up around them. Typically, as at Dereham, there were granaries, maltings, the gas works and a steam mill. Any industry relying on coal or iron was also likely to be near the railway line.

A unique feature of the Norfolk countryside, created by the railway age, is the 'railway village' of Melton Constable. Alien to the surrounding rural area, it did not develop secondary industries and instead relied on the railway for its survival. Built on virgin soil bought from Lord Hastings by the Midland and Great Northern Joint Railway Company, its population grew from 118 in 1881 to 1,157 in 1911. Between 1881 and

92. A train coming into Hethersett station.

93. Fakenham station, opened in 1859.

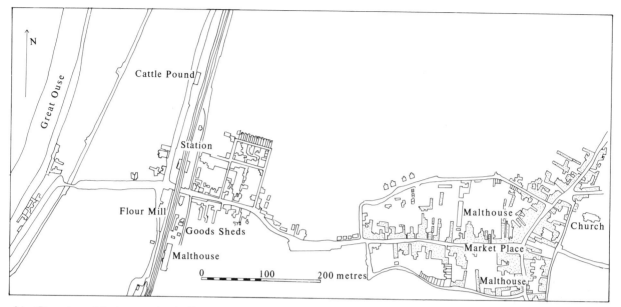

94. Downham Market was in decline as a market town in the early 19th century, but the opening of the railway in 1882 led to the development of an industrial area with a flour mill and malt houses near the station. The medieval core of the town, stippled on the map, was very sparsely built up by 1900, with many gaps behind and amongst the buildings.

95. Watton was one of Norfolk's smaller and slower growing market towns. Although it was the terminus of a coach route and toll road until the 1840s, it was not linked to the railway (via Thetford) until the end of the century. However, as soon as a station was opened, a small industrial settlement, including a foundry, grew up nearby and houses were built along the road between the old town, stippled on the map, and the station. The town also began to expand westwards from the wide High Street, used as a market place.

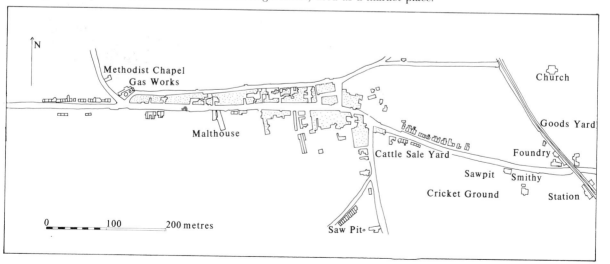

1883, the first 28 houses were built along Melton Street, followed by the railway works in a style more typical of the late 19th-century artisan house of the Midlands than of anything usually found in Norfolk. In 1886 a second group of houses known as Astley Terrace was erected and there was further major expansion in the 1890s. All the houses were supplied with gas and running water, while a grocer's shop, a doctor, allotments and a recreation ground were all provided by the railway company.

Most market towns had a station by 1900, even if only on a branch line, and entered the 20th century with busy markets and a variety of industries; their future appeared to be assured and their role, serving the local community, had changed little since the Middle Ages.

Into a New Century

In contrast to the first half of the 19th century, the appearance of the countryside changed very little in the early years of the twentieth. Depressed agricultural prices ensured that any woods, commons and heathland which had survived the years of high farming remained intact until at least the end of the Second World War. Only men such as James Keith, whose family like many others had come to Norfolk from Scotland at the end of the 19th century, had the optimism to bring new land into cultivation; in the 1930s, 1,000 acres of Harpley Common, Massingham Heath and Massingham Common were cleared of gorse, bracken and rabbits, and, by deep ploughing, manuring and heavy liming, made to produce good cereal crops.

96. By 1914, much of the countryside had a neglected air, with a minimum being invested in repair. Very little has been spent on this field barn and cattle sheds in Aldeby since 1870.

Farm buildings, too, were altered little until after 1945. Most had been built in the prosperous years before 1870 and, with little being spent on maintenance, were very dilapidated by the 1930s. Work on maintaining hedges and keeping crops free of weeds was also kept to a minimum to reduce overheads, so much of the countryside had an overgrown and uncared for appearance. Keith took on a farm in 1935 that had been let go in this way: 'I thought that if at some time it had given a living to an English family, it could at least help keep a thrifty Scot.' However, many farmers did fail and there were whole pages in the *Eastern Daily Press* devoted to farm sales.

Although the landscape remained unchanged, social developments during the first half of the 20th century were considerable. The First World War is often seen as a turning point for the countryside. For the first time, large numbers of countrymen left their own county and met others from all over Britain. They learned of an alternative life style which could be lived in the towns and many never returned to the countryside. In some villages a whole generation either died in battle or found a life elsewhere.

The war had a shortlived stimulating affect on agriculture as the supply of food from overseas was disrupted by German submarines, and for the first time the government took some control over agricultural production and wages. Farmers were compelled to pay a minimum wage of 25 shillings a week and the voice of the National Agricultural Labourers' and Rural Workers' Union was heard at county negotiating level. Farm labourers were no longer the subservient group they had been for much of the previous century.

The upper as well as the lower ranks of society were affected by the great changes in the social order which were sweeping across Britain after 1918. The whole basis on which the countryside had functioned was altered by the selling up of estates, partly as a result of the long years of depression and partly because of the introduction of death duties by the post-war Liberal government. Families that had controlled great tracts of countryside for several hundred years, such as the Earls of Leicester, the Earls of Albemarle at Quiddenham, Lord Suffield at Gunton and the Evans-Lombes at Bylaugh, sold off varying proportions of their estates, often to their tenant farmers. The landlord-tenant system which had dominated agriculture for so long began to be broken throughout Norfolk.

With the old landed families leaving the great houses, and labourers leaving their cottages for the towns, the character of the countryside began to change. This was accelerated by the arrival of the motorbus. Before 1914 there had been a bus service between Yarmouth and Lowestoft, but in 1919 E. B. Hutchinson extended his enterprise by introducing a bus between Norwich and Aylsham, carrying on to Cromer in the summer. The business was a success from the start and was soon extended to cover the whole county under the name of United Automobile Services Ltd. The isolation and self-sufficiency of the village, which the railway and the bicycle had done so much to break down, were now finally gone.

In spite of the agricultural depression, there were some changes in farming practice. With low grain prices, less and less land was used for arable crops. Some 5,000 acres a year became pasture between 1918 and 1923 and the increased demand for milk encouraged a change to dairy farming in many areas, particularly on the heavier clays. The arrival of Scottish dairy farmers and their Ayrshire cows in the 1920s ensured that Norfolk became an important milk producing county with a large surplus going to London every day.

The cultivation of soft fruits continued to increase, particularly in the Broads and the Fens. This was encouraged by the setting up of Norfolk County Council's Horticultural Station at Burlingham in 1920 where demonstrations were held. An advertising campaign by the Fruit Growing Association encouraged sales; the establishment of jam pulp and canning factories in Wisbech, Kings Lynn, Thetford, North

Walsham, Yarmouth and Lowestoft, as well as cider-making at Attleborough, also provided a steady market. Blackcurrants, cherries, apples and pears all became well-established crops.

By far the most important new crop was sugar beet. It was grown on many farms, but there was no sugar beet factory in England, so until 1912 the crop had to be sent to Holland. There were many advantages to this new crop; it could replace turnips and mangolds in the rotation sequence but, unlike them, it was a cash crop so yarded bullocks and folded sheep did not have to be fed on the roots before there could be any return on the crop. Sugar beet provided a way out of the agricultural depression, with the first sugar beet factory being established at Cantley in 1912.

The main change to be seen in Norfolk farming in the inter-war years was a break from the four-course system, involving the keeping of large numbers of sheep and cattle, to fewer livestock combined with an increasing acreage of sugar beet. Some farmers were also growing fruit, vegetables and potatoes. However, profit margins were uniformly low and, with the disappearance of sheep and later horses, less labour was needed. Farming techniques continued much as before. The lack of profits was a disincentive to change and, although tractors were available, few found their way onto Norfolk farms before the 1930s.

Agriculture continued to be the major employer throughout most of Norfolk. In the fenland area of west Norfolk between 60 and 70 per cent of the employed population worked in agriculture as late as 1921. Throughout most of the county the proportion was over 50 per cent. Vegetables were the most labour-intensive and were grown in the Fens and the Broads where one person was employed to every two acres of cultivated land. Over much of the rest of the county, one person to every three acres was employed while only on the very light soils was the figure as low as one person for every four acres. The dramatic decline in the number of farm labourers did not really begin until after 1940 with the replacement of the horse by the tractor.

The stagnation of agriculture in the early part of the century was reflected in the market towns which relied on local farmers for their trade. Industries such as iron foundries, which flourished on war-time contracts, often floundered after 1918 and many went out of business, though Cranes of Dereham is a notable exception to this general rule. As a result of the increase in imported grain, local water mills closed. Railways encouraged the introduction of new industries geared to a national rather than a local market, and new factories were set up in some of the larger towns. The smaller towns, however, declined and very little building took place in the inter-war period.

Although in many ways life in the countryside continued much as it had always done, the First World War was a social watershed and marked the end of the rigid distinction between landlord and tenant farmer which had been the hallmark of the 19th century. As the rural population declined, the bargaining position of the farm labourer improved, although he still had a long way to go before his wages equalled those paid to industrial workers. The real change in farming fortunes did not come until after the Second World War with the end of horse husbandry and the beginning of farm subsidies which made farming the prosperous and highly mechanised industry it is today.

The countryside is now facing another period of change in its turbulent history. Increasing car ownership has made it possible for the town worker to live further and

97, 98 & 99. First World War Land Army girls working on J. Thisteton Smith's farm at West Barsham: enrolling a member of the Land Army (*above*); chopping turnips (*opposite above*); feeding bullocks in yards (*opposite below*).

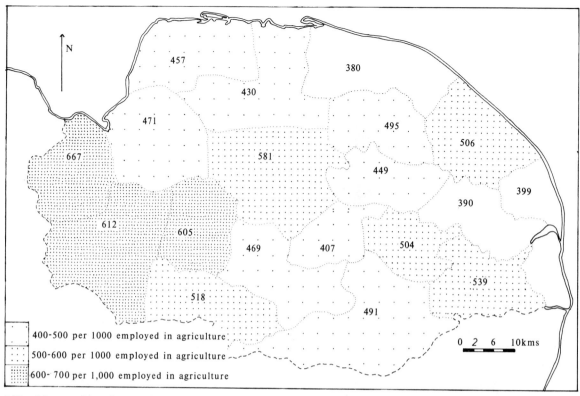

100. Map to show the number of people employed in agriculture for every 1,000 acres cultivated in 1921. Figures are given per Rural District Council.

101. Map to show the percentage of population employed in agriculture in 1921. The figures are given per Rural District Council.

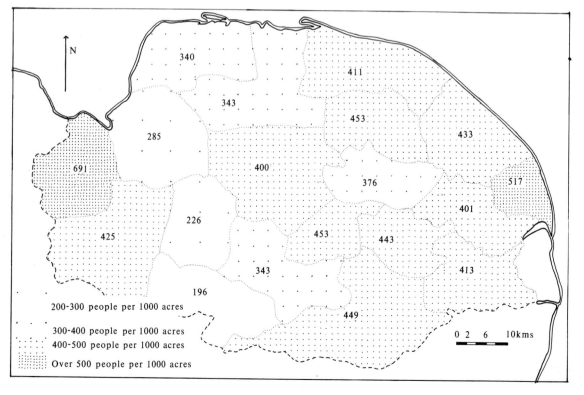

102. War memorial in Castle Acre churchyard. Forty-one names are listed with as many as four from one family. This must have been a very high percentage of the young males from a village with a total population of just over 1,000 in 1911.

further away from his work in the countryside. As a result, since 1950, the process of population decline has been reversed in all but the remotest communities. This increasingly affluent new rural society has brought enormous changes in the villages. Not old enough or architecturally interesting enough to merit conservation, old village schools and chapels are derelict or converted into houses. Village shops are either closed or encased in modern plastic shop fronts. Farm buildings, dating from the Napoleonic war grain boom and the later period of 'high farming', survived the years of depression, but are now obsolete and often unsuitable for conversion by progressive farmers; they too are being demolished or converted into houses. Hedges and woods are removed and wetlands drained to increase cereal output. Roads are straightened and villages bypassed.

In these and many other respects the countryside is changing more dramatically than it ever did in the 19th century and the visual evidence for a whole way of life is being engulfed in housing estates or is being removed to create grain prairies. Norfolk's population is now one of the fastest growing in the United Kingdom. Although this brings much-needed investment to what has been a rural backwater, it is all the more important that an awareness of the past should be the basis of planning for the future.

Select Bibliography

Chapter One

Green, B. and Young, R. M. K., *Norwich, the Growth of a City* (1964)
Hawkins, C. B., *Norwich; a social study* (1910)
Young, R., 'The Norwich Chartists' in *Chartism in East Anglia* (unpublished typescript, 1951)

Chapter Two

Berry, V., *The Rolfe Papers: The Chronicles of a Norfolk family, 1559-1908* (1979)
Girouard, M., *The Victorian Country House* (1971)
Haggard, H. R., *A Farmer's Year* (1899)
Harbord, C., Baron Suffield, *My Memories, 1830-1913* (1913)
Hayes, B. D., 'Politics in Norfolk, 1752-1832' (unpublished Ph.D. thesis, Cambridge, 1957)
Kent, N., *General View of the Agriculture of the County of Norfolk* (1794)
Ketton-Cremer, R. W., *Felbrigg: the Story of a House* (1962)
Marshall, W., *The Rural Economy of Norfolk*, 2 vols. (1787)
Parker, R. H. C., *Coke of Norfolk and the Agricultural Revolution* (1975)
Pevsner, N., *Buildings of England: North-east Norfolk and Norwich* (1962) and *North-west and South Norfolk* (1962)
Stirling, A. M. W., *Coke of Norfolk and his Friends*, 2 vols. (1908)
Wade Martins, S., *A Great Estate at Work* (1980)
Winkley, G., *The Country Houses of Norfolk* (1986)

Chapter Three

Bacon, R. N., *The Agriculture of Norfolk* (1844)
Faden, W., *Map of Norfolk*, reprint by Norfolk Record Society, Vol.47 (1973)
Kent, N., *op. cit.*
Marshall, W., *op. cit.*
Parker, R. H. C., *op. cit.*
Stirling, A. M. W., *op. cit.*
Wade Martins, S., *op. cit.*
Young, A., *A General View of the Agriculture of the County of Norfolk* (1804)
Yaxley, D. (ed.), *Survey of Houghton Hall Estate, 1800*, Norfolk Record Society, Vol. 50 (1984)

Chapter Four

Haggard, H. R., *op. cit.*
Haggard, H. R., *Rural England*, 2 vols. (1902)
Read, C. S., 'Agriculture of Norfolk' in White, W., *Directory of Norfolk* (1883)
Wade Martins, S., *op. cit.*

Chapter Five

Crowley, J. and Reid, A. (eds), *The Poor Law in Norfolk, 1700-1850; a collection of source material* (1983)
Digby, A., *Pauper Palaces* (1978)
Edwards, G., *From Crowscaring to Westminster* (1922)
Evans, G. E., *Ask the Fellows who cut the Hay* (1956)
Evans, G. E., *The Horse in the Furrow* (1960)
Evans, G. E., *The Pattern under the Plough* (1966)

Evans, G. E., *The Farm and the Village* (1969)
Evans, G. E., *Where Beards Wag All* (1970)
Evans, G. E., *The Days we have seen* (1975)
Groves, R., *Sharpen the Sickle! The History of the Farm Workers' Union* (1949)
Haggard, L. R., *I walked by night* (1935)
Haggard, L. R., *The Rabbitskin Cap* (1939)
Hobsbawm, E. J., and Rude, G., *Captain Swing* (1969)
Howkins, A., *Poor Labouring Men, Rural Radicalism in Norfolk, 1872-1923* (1985)
Jessopp, A., *Arcady, for better, for worse* (1887)
Livingstone, S., *A Penny a Boy* (1978)
Norfolk Federation of Women's Institutes, *Within Living Memory: A Collection of Norfolk Reminiscences* (1971)
Peacock, A. J., *Bread or Blood: a Study of the Agrarian Riots in East Anglia in 1816* (1965)
Scotland, N. A. D., 'Methodism and the Revolt of the Field in East Anglia, 1872-96' in *Wesley Hist. Soc. Proceedings* (1981)
Springall, M., *Labouring Life in Norfolk Villages, 1834-1914* (1936)

Chapter Six

Armstrong, B. J., *Norfolk Diary* (1949 and 1963)
Chadwick, O., *A Victorian Miniature* (1961)
Jessopp, A., *op. cit.*
Jolly, C., *The Spreading Flame. The Coming of Methodism to Norfolk, 1751-1811* (1973)
Ladbrooke, R., *Views of the Churches of Norfolk*, 5 vols. (1843)
Norfolk Federation of Women's Institutes, *op. cit.*
Scotland, N. A. D., *op. cit.*
Springall, M., *op. cit.*
Yaxley, D., *op. cit.*

Chapter Seven

Armstrong, B. J., *op. cit.*
Boston, N., and Puddy, E., *Dereham: the Biography of a Country Town* (1952)
Crosby, A., *A History of Thetford* (1986)
Gordon, D. I., *A Regional History of the Railways of Great Britain: vol 5, The Eastern Counties* (1968)
Sapwell, J., *A History of Aylsham* (1960)

Chapter Eight

Newby, H., *This Green and Pleasant Land?* (1979)

General Titles

Hepworth, P., *Victorian and Edwardian Norfolk from old photographs* (1972)
Mardle, J., *Victorian Norfolk* (1981)
Wade-Martins, P. (ed), *Norfolk from the Air*
Wade Martins, S., *A History of Norfolk* (1984)

Index